HowExpert Guide to Cats

101 Tips to Learn How to Get, Take Care of, Raise, and Love Cats as a Cat Guardian

HowExpert with Crystal Rector

For more tips related to this topic, visit HowExpert.com/cat.

Recommended Resources

- HowExpert.com – Quick 'How To' Guides on All Topics from A to Z by Everyday Experts.
- HowExpert.com/free – Free HowExpert Email Newsletter.
- HowExpert.com/books – HowExpert Books
- HowExpert.com/courses – HowExpert Courses
- HowExpert.com/clothing – HowExpert Clothing
- HowExpert.com/membership – HowExpert Membership Site
- HowExpert.com/affiliates – HowExpert Affiliate Program
- HowExpert.com/jobs – HowExpert Jobs
- HowExpert.com/writers – Write About Your #1 Passion/Knowledge/Expertise & Become a HowExpert Author.
- HowExpert.com/resources – Additional HowExpert Recommended Resources
- YouTube.com/HowExpert – Subscribe to HowExpert YouTube.
- Instagram.com/HowExpert – Follow HowExpert on Instagram.
- Facebook.com/HowExpert – Follow HowExpert on Facebook.
- TikTok.com/@HowExpert – Follow HowExpert on TikTok.

Publisher's Foreword

Dear HowExpert Reader,

HowExpert publishes quick 'how to' guides on all topics from A to Z by everyday experts.

At HowExpert, our mission is to discover, empower, and maximize everyday people's talents to ultimately make a positive impact in the world for all topics from A to Z...one everyday expert at a time!

All of our HowExpert guides are written by everyday people just like you and me, who have a passion, knowledge, and expertise for a specific topic.

We take great pride in selecting everyday experts who have a passion, real-life experience in a topic, and excellent writing skills to teach you about the topic you are also passionate about and eager to learn.

We hope you get a lot of value from our HowExpert guides, and it can make a positive impact on your life in some way. All of our readers, including you, help us continue living our mission of positively impacting the world for all spheres of influences from A to Z.

If you enjoyed one of our HowExpert guides, then please take a moment to send us your feedback from wherever you got this book.

Thank you, and we wish you all the best in all aspects of life.

Sincerely,

BJ Min
Founder & Publisher of HowExpert
HowExpert.com

PS...If you are also interested in becoming a HowExpert author, then please visit our website at HowExpert.com/writers. Thank you & again, all the best!

Table of Contents

Introduction

Dear reader and prospective cat guardian, welcome to your expert guide to sharing your life with a cat – or ideally, with multiple cats. This guide will take you from beginning to end and from simple to more complex and will provide you with 101 Tips and Tricks to ensure you and your feline friend(s) live long, happy, and healthy lives together.

The intention here is to help you be the best you can be for your cat, and that is perhaps a tall order, but I believe in you and your ability and willingness to fully commit to giving your best to the new feline friend with whom you will share a home. Otherwise, you would not be reading this book in the first place.

Tip #1: Keep your mind open to learning and maintain a strong commitment to your cat's wellbeing.

In that spirit, I will warn you that some of the ideas and opinions I express may seem a bit foreign to you or even run counter to traditional beliefs you may have picked up along the way in this ride we call life. However, my philosophies on raising happy and healthy cats are more cutting edge than traditional, keeping with the most current information and trends among feline behaviorists, nutritionists, and other experts on all things cat-related. Therefore, I ask you to read with an open mind and try applying the principles I share with you before deciding it's not for you. I promise you your cat is worth the effort.

The phrasing I will be using here when referring to you and your cat is a very deliberate reflection of the respect for your cat – and for cats in general – that I wish to inspire in you. This author believes that words matter, and they expose and shape attitudes.

Therefore, I choose never to use the pronoun "it" to describe a cat, just as I would not refer to a person as it. It refers to inanimate objects and not to living, breathing, sentient beings with feelings. Obviously, I do not know the gender of your cat or cats, but I will use he/him, she/her, and they/them in a more general sense as those pronouns can be used interchangeably about most topics.

Likewise, I avoid terms such as "pet" (in its noun form) and "owner," as these words carry with them a connotation of human superiority. All souls are equal and do not fall on a hierarchical continuum of importance or value. We all occupy different types of bodies and therefore have different types of life experiences. We experience our lives from a human standpoint, while our cats experience theirs through the lens of a feline perspective.

In full disclosure, the hypocrisy is not lost on me of my ownership of a business that includes the word "pet" in it. I am conflicted about this because it does not reflect my evolved current philosophy about using terminology that places human and non-human animals in a hierarchy of value.

I have been using my business name since 2012, approximately nine years ago as I write this. As humans, we should all strive to continue growing and learning, and that is especially true of those who represent themselves as experts in any field. As a person who works with animals, I endeavor to continue my education and growth in the animal care industry, and my current opinion and feelings on the matter reflect that evolution.

The change of heart I have about my business name is a direct result of that continual advancement. I am currently mulling over potential new business names. Still, I am finding it tricky to find a concise title that expresses the concept of substitute caretaker of companion animals which omits the commonly used term "pet," so for now, the name remains the same. But, again, the hypocrisy is not lost on me.

You, dear reader, are getting the opportunity to start fresh from this more advanced perspective. When we bring a cat into our home, we take on the responsibility for that feline life. We become the source of everything the cat needs. Since this is a dynamic similar to a parent and child relationship, intermixed with terms such as cat guardian and cat caretaker, I will sometimes refer to readers as cat parents as well.

With that foundation in place, let's now embark on a journey together to achieve the best lifelong relationship between you and your cat.

Chapter 1: Preparing to Add a Cat to Your Family

As any journalist can tell you, every good and complete investigation follows a pattern of discovery to include the five "w's" and an "h." Specifically, and in no particular order, these include: Who, What, Where, When, Why, and How.

Tip #2: Think ahead and prepare before jumping into cat guardianship.

Thinking ahead to your future with any new family member should include careful thought and thorough preparation, and it is no different with a new cat. Therefore, we will answer a set of such questions before we even get off the ground.

Why Add a Cat to Your Family?

If you are considering adding a cat or a kitten to your family, then let me be the first to congratulate you. You are making a decision to enrich a feline life and the lives of the rest of your family as well, even if you are the only other member of the household.

The benefits of cat guardianship are numerous and profound. Science proves the health benefits of living with cats. Just being around them lowers stress levels in humans, improving our health in various ways, from preventing heart disease and strokes to improving our sleep patterns. Simply engaging in petting a cat gives us a boost of oxytocin, a hormone associated with bonding and reducing anxiety and stress.

Whoever first presented the age-old adage about laughter being the best medicine may have had a cat in their life and could speak with authority about the healing properties of laughter from the silly antics of a cat at play. It is undoubtedly the primary reason for the proliferation of hilarious cat videos on the internet. After all, even the most irritable among us must admit feeling delight from watching a cat riding atop a robot vacuum or playing patty-cake with another cat (both are videos you can find online with a quick search if you are interested and want a laugh).

Anyone who has experienced the soothing feeling of being around a purring cat can attest to the calming effect of the sound and vibration on their mood. However, purring has another, more unexpected benefit as well. Cats use the power of the purr for self-soothing and to express contentment or to request something from their human benefactors. They also use it for physical healing.

The vibratory frequency range at which cats purr is scientifically recognized to assist in healing masses such as bone, muscles, and tendons. It is valid for helping to heal the purring cat but also holds true for us. Following an injury, you might do well to have a cat purring in your presence to help speed the healing process.

Another health benefit that may seem counter-intuitive to some is a potential for allergy reduction for children exposed to cats and other animals when very young. For example, studies find that kids exposed to a cat before their first birthday have a lower risk of developing a range of common allergies, including allergies to cats and extending to substances such as plant pollens and dust mites.

A love of cats might even improve our relationships with other humans. Scientific research indicates that people who share their lives with cats tend to have higher levels of trust in others and behave with more sensitivity toward others compared to the poor souls whose lives are cat deprived. It makes sense in the context of connectivity.

People who feel connected with another being increase their capacity for positive social qualities such as generosity and compassion. Research conducted in Scotland found that children who interact well with best human friends tend to have a strong attachment to their best feline friends, suggesting a correlation between bonding with human and non-human animals.

Tip #3: Two cats are better than one!

The previous tips are great benefits for the humans who are contemplating opening up their homes to a cat - or better yet, to more than one. But, of course, the cats profit from this symbiotic relationship as well.

According to data from the ASPCA (Association for the Prevention of Cruelty to Animals), over three million cats enter the animal shelter system annually. Of those, more than two and a half million healthy cats are killed to make room for new cats needing to gain access to the shelter. Therefore, for each cat you bring into your home, you save two lives: the one you bring home and the one who will take his place.

Even the cats languishing in no-kill shelters stand to benefit from your choosing to bring them home. Contrary to popular belief, cats are social creatures, and they often break down both physically and emotionally from being caged in a shelter for long periods.

Opening your home to a new feline family member gets the cat out of a wholly unnatural environment and into a much healthier family setting. In a home, she can experience the love and interaction that she needs to flourish into the creature she was born to be.

When is the Best Time to Add a Cat to Your Family?

As we've established, cats are living beings with needs and identities all their own, so it's essential to seriously consider the fitness of your home and family life for a new feline inhabitant before plunging full speed ahead. It is a relationship that should not be approached impulsively.

Tip #4: Have a home fit for feline inhabitants before bringing a cat into it.

Therefore, the best time to add a cat to your family is after you've done all your research, and you have concluded that you and the rest of your household are "all in" – willing to commit time, energy, and resources to the new family member for the duration of the cat's life, not just through the "cute kitten" phase.

Remember that the novelty of having this feline in your life will eventually wear off. As cats have been known to live well into their thirties, the commitment may be very long in terms of the sheer number of years.

Tip #5: Be sure you are up to the challenge before you commit.

The average feline lifespan is admittedly significantly shorter than it was for the current record-holder, Crème Puff, who lived just over 38 years. Typically, indoor cats live into their teens and twenties, but you should be aware before beginning your time with this new family member that with proper care, your cat's lifespan has the potential to go the distance.

If, after conducting your research, you feel confident that you are willing and able to support the cat until the end of his life, then this may be the perfect time to begin your beautiful relationship with a feline friend.

What to Consider About Adding a Cat to Your Family?

Okay, so you are ready to do your research but unsure where to begin or what kinds of considerations you even need to make. We are here to help you with that, as there are some important considerations before you jump into the cat-caring waters. We touched a bit on commitment in the previous section, but let's dive a little more deeply into what that means.

The first consideration that comes to mind is the expense. Commonly, people think only about the initial adoption or purchase cost and feeding when they budget for adding an animal to their families. Still, such expenses are just the tip of the iceberg when it comes to investment in a feline companion.

Tip #6: Take an honest assessment of your finances to evaluate whether or not you can truly afford to take proper care of a cat.

Supplies

Cats need supplies such as bowls for their food and water, litter pans and litter, brushes and combs, toys and other enrichment items, a suitable cat carrier, perhaps a leash and an identification collar or harness and tag, as well as local licensing. These are just basic supplies, which will likely need to be replaced several times throughout the cat's lifetime.

Travel

Tip #7: Research the average cost for a professional sitter for your cat, rather than relying on friends, family members, or the neighbor kid.

If you travel for business or pleasure, you should budget for the expense of a good reliable sitter to take care of your friend while you are away. Skimping in this department can have disastrous results, as you often get what you pay for in terms of sitters.

Find a sitter who will spend time with your cat in your absence, rather than simply dropping by to quickly pour some food in a bowl and scoop a litter box. Someone who either specializes in cats or has a keen understanding of feline nature is preferable. In addition, a professional who carries pet-sitting insurance will give you extra peace of mind.

Alternatively, if your cat will travel with you, as some people choose in certain circumstances, you should factor in hotel companion animal fees. For air travel, you will encounter additional costs for bringing your cat along as well.

Health Care

A more significant expense – and one that often takes people by surprise – is the cost of veterinary care. Even routine veterinary care can be pretty expensive, but that expense can skyrocket very quickly in the case of illness or injury.

Please keep in mind that although veterinary clinics and hospitals are technically businesses, the doctors and staff really love animals, and they enter the animal care industry because of that love for animals.

Tip #8: Understand that most veterinarians are not price-gouging when they charge what they need to charge to pay their bills – although consumers sometimes have the perception that they are.

Medical treatment is expensive, whether it is a medical treatment for humans or animals. However, because of the perceived lower value of animals in relation to humans, veterinarians are not able to charge as much as human doctors do.

Keep in mind that the amount of education, the techniques, and the equipment and supplies they need to use are usually comparable or even the same as for their human physician counterparts. These are expenses that they need to recover to stay in business and be available to treat your cat.

Tip #9: Consider investing in health insurance and/or a wellness care plan your veterinarian may offer for your cat.

Health Insurance

For human medicine, health insurance usually helps to defray the costs to the consumer, which drives up the overall price of medical treatments for humans and animals as pharmaceutical and medical supply companies increase their prices accordingly, and veterinarians are forced to increase treatment costs.

Most animal health insurance is different from human health insurance. It is less apt to cover significant chunks of your cat's medical costs than what you may be accustomed to having your own insurance cover. Understand that your cat's medical expenses could be significant, and when you welcome her into your family, you also take on the responsibility to keep her healthy.

Although the billing structures for animal health insurance differ from the human equivalent, the premiums do cost less, and insurance can be a godsend in the case of a catastrophic emergency. Unlike human health insurance, most animal health insurance plans do not cover animals with preexisting conditions, and they often charge more for senior animals. These facts increase the benefit of beginning coverage earlier.

Wellness Plans

In addition to health insurance, some veterinarians offer wellness plans to defray some costs of routine preventative veterinary care. These plans bundle services that are recommended for regular treatment into a package with a reduced overall cost. It's sort of like ordering a full meal at a restaurant rather than requesting each dish ala carte. Such plans are especially common for kittens to encourage a healthy start to life and can help to lower the overall cost of keeping your cat vigorous and fit.

Living Situations

Another consideration that people frequently overlook is the permanence or stability of their living situation. For example, you may currently live in a place that will welcome your cat with open arms, but many rental properties do not allow cats.

Those who allow cats often require extra deposits and monthly "pet rent," which increases your housing costs. Suppose there is a possibility you may need to move before the end of your cat's life. In that case, you should be cognizant that you will need to find housing that will allow you to keep the kitty with you and that there might be additional costs associated with your feline roommate.

Tip #10: Be prepared for housing challenges if you rent. If there is a possibility you may need to move, research cat-friendly housing ahead of time.

A common reason that people give for surrendering cats to shelters is the need to move and the rules at the new place disallowing cats to live on the premises. This kind of circumstance is wholly unfair to the innocent cat, having had no choice in the matter and having done nothing to deserve abandonment. Forethought and pre-planning on your part will prevent a scenario in which you need to find appropriate housing for you and your kitty in the future.

Family Planning

Tip #11: Consider your future family planning.

Another common reason people give for abandoning cats at shelters involves new household members, whether that means a new significant other has come into the picture or a new baby is due, or the family wants to add a dog.

None of these are valid reasons for leaving your cat behind, but they are much too frequently treated as such. Again, it is entirely unfair to abandon any family member, including your feline friend. If you can imagine this kind of scenario, you should reconsider adding a cat to your family until your commitment to the cat is solid.

Lifestyle

Your lifestyle might be another consideration. For example, while it's true that cats are "independent" – meaning they are capable of survival in an outdoor, human-free setting when necessary, it's also true that they are social and prone to loneliness, anxiety, and boredom when left alone for long periods, especially inside a home where they are trapped in an environment not necessarily conducive to their natural behaviors.

In the wild, housecats form colonies, working together for the good of each individual. It is a bit of a misconception that cats prefer to be alone. They are actually naturally communal, and they even nurse kittens communally within their colonies. Like humans, some cats tend to be introverted, and others are more socially outgoing. However, either way, being completely alone in your home for long spells can be very stressful.

Tip #12: If you lead a lifestyle that often has you away from home for long stretches, you should consider the impact it will have on your little house feline.

For some cats, such a situation might be tolerable with a good sitter and/or another cat in the house. However, for other cats, it could become a source of high anxiety. Therefore, for your cat's wellbeing, it's a good idea to take an honest assessment of your situation before bringing a cat into your household.

Allergies

Even allergies can be a necessary consideration. For example, some people have severe allergies to cat dander and have serious reactions when exposed to cats. However, if such a problem presents, it does not need to mean you cannot continue to share your home and your life with your cat.

Tip #13: It is incumbent on you to find solutions that work for both the allergic party and the cat.

"Hypoallergenic" Cats

There is a persistent myth that some cat breeds are hypoallergenic, but sadly, this is not true; at least, it is not true in its strictest sense. The mechanism that causes an allergic reaction in some people is a protein that is present within the cat, primarily in the sebaceous glands and saliva.

As cats groom themselves, they spread it all over their coat, and the resulting dander can cause various physical reactions from very mild to very severe in humans. This protein, known as FEL-D1, is naturally lower in some individual cats than in others, and in some breeds, it is more likely to be lower, but that is no guarantee.

Sometimes it is simply a matter of testing an individual cat and human combination to find out whether or not they can coexist. Some people will have an intense response to one cat and hardly react at all to another. In the case of a strong reaction, there are some ways to cope and reduce the miserable symptoms.

Allergen-Reducing Cat Diets

An exciting recent breakthrough in the cat food space is a diet you can feed to your cat that will reduce the amount of FEL-D1 in your cat, therefore reducing the amount of allergen your cat produces. As this novel dietary solution is proven over time, all the various cat food brands will likely begin offering diets with a similar feature, giving you and your cat more choices in the future.

Grooming Solutions

Also helpful for reducing the allergy-inducing dander in the environment is to brush your cat often, reducing the need for your cat to groom herself and taking some of the existing dander out of the environment. Of course, she will still groom because that's what cats do, but the cleaner she feels, the less compelled she will feel to tidy her coat.

Please do not misinterpret this as a suggestion that you bathe your cat. As cats are designed to clean themselves, they rarely need help in bathing. For you to frequently bathe your cat will likely result in dry skin, which may exacerbate the dander problem (and frighten or anger your cat!).

Housekeeping and Cat-Free Spaces

Finally, keeping an extra-clean house can help reduce the dander floating around. If you usually dust and vacuum your home weekly, you might find it helps to do so twice weekly or more. If all else fails, keeping a section of the house cat-free for the allergic party might be necessary. Allergists sometimes suggest the allergic person sleep in a cat-free space for the best results.

Where Should You Find Your New Family Member?

People acquire cats in different ways, and this can be a crucial choice for several reasons. The issue of sourcing your new cat can have both ethical and practical consequences that you might want to think about before deciding, so we'll cover the various potential sources with their pros and cons.

Outdoor Rescue

Some people find that they do not need to put effort into finding a cat. The cat comes to them and wants to become part of the family. Perhaps he shows up at the front door, meowing for help and food. Who can resist a poor kitty in need – or an insistent cry for help?

Adopting this way serves to get the cat out of the undesirable situation of living on the street and can help prevent unwanted litters of kittens if the cat has not yet been altered. It also helps the adopter feel good for providing a home to a needy soul.

Of course, this kind of circumstance would happen without any pre-planning or preparation, too. Just be sure to think through your decision thoroughly and do some research before you commit. Be aware that you do not know the background or health of the cat, and you could be taking on significant responsibility, so be sure you are prepared for that.

Tip #14: Do not force a feral cat to live in your home, but do provide for his needs outdoors.

If the cat you see outdoors appears to be feral – lacking positive social experience with humans – bringing the cat into your home is likely a bad idea. A truly wild cat will generally never be happy inside a human home and will live his life in fear, even if you have the best and purest intentions.

That does not mean you cannot still care for the cat. You can provide outdoor shelter, food, water, and veterinary care without forcing the cat to live unhappily indoors. They may even eventually warm up to you and choose to come inside.

Historically speaking, it is possible to rehabilitate a feral cat to live comfortably indoors, but you would need the proper household, infinite patience, and expertise to pull off that trick. But, of course, that would encompass a separate book altogether!

Pet Store or Online Classified Purchase

Tip #15: Avoid buying from pet stores or online classified listings.

Some people go shopping for a cat because they have a specific idea of the kind of cat they want or because they see a cute kitten in a store window and fall in love. Animal-lovers in the know cringe at this idea for several reasons.

First, and perhaps most importantly, kittens from stores are usually the sad byproduct of the animal mill industry. Some people are familiar with the term "puppy mill" and are surprised to learn that kitten mills are also common (as are rabbit, ferret, guinea pig, chinchilla, and other various rodent mills).

Animal mills sell their "product" through stores and online classified venues such as Craig's List. Anytime a store or classified outlet is selling an animal that a reputable rescue organization does not back up, that animal is a likely victim of an animal mill: a business that profits from breeding animals without regard to the health and wellness of the individuals being bred.

Mass production of animals leads to overbreeding, which harms the mother animals, which are forced to bear litter after litter without relief. Also, the conditions in which the animals are forced to live while at the mill, which is basically a large-scale breeding farm, are crowded, unsanitary, and generally unhealthful.

Purchasing an animal that comes from a mill presents a moral dilemma. On the one hand, the kitten has likely already experienced horrific conditions in her short life, and you could be the one to bring her to a loving home.

On the other hand, your purchasing her only serves to support the unethical kitten mill industry. If there is no market for kittens bred this way, the industry will collapse and die out. If people continue to buy kittens this way, however, the industry will continue operating with impunity.

Additionally, because she came from an unhealthy environment, your kitten could be harboring illnesses, disorders, or inherited "defects" that are not immediately obvious. Providing veterinary care to ill or injured animals is unprofitable to the breeder, so mill animals are often sold with untreated illnesses and underlying conditions. Because unethical breeders lack concerns about the ultimate health of their final "products" and care only about financial gain, inbreeding is also common, leading to congenital health problems.

An animal coming from such a dubious background comes with a higher likelihood of becoming very sick and even dying shortly following your purchase. She could also potentially pose a risk to humans and other animals in your household, bringing viral, bacterial, fungal, or parasitic pathogens into your home.

Backyard Breeder

Tip #16: Adopting an animal from a backyard breeder is risky.

Occasionally you might come across someone selling kittens from their own home or on the side of the road, outside a store, etc. Generally speaking, these are not large-scale operations like a kitten mill. Sometimes they are a smaller-scale version of the same, trying to make money from the sale of a litter or two of kittens at a time. It is admittedly a less insidious situation than a full-on animal mill but is still an ethical concern. Had this litter not been born, a litter's worth of homeless kittens could have otherwise been rescued.

Often, such operations result from people failing to take precautions like spaying and neutering their animals, resulting in an unwanted litter. In addition, they might have purposely allowed their cat to become pregnant in a misguided attempt to provide an educational experience to their children or to keep one of her kittens and give the rest away. Unfortunately, these are all fairly common scenarios.

To give them the benefit of the doubt, in some cases, they may have taken in a stray mama cat off the street and provided her shelter so she could birth her babies or some similar situation. But, regardless of the reason, you take a chance that the kitten may not be healthy when you take him home, as these people are operating informally and, in some cases, perhaps even illegally.

Similar to a kitten mill baby, your new friend's background is questionable, and he might have contagious health issues or possibly even congenital problems from inbreeding. You take that risk when obtaining a kitten from a backyard breeder.

Responsible Breeder

We cannot disparage all cat breeders as irresponsible. Some breed their cats very carefully to avoid genetic mutations and promote the best health in their cats. Responsible breeders generally do not profit from the sale of their cats as they invest quite a bit financially and emotionally into providing upscale care.

Regardless of the better care given to cats bred responsibly, there still remains an ethical component to consider. These people are generally breeding purebred cats for showing at cat shows.

Qualities that make a cat "perfect" in terms of cat show requisites are still relatively difficult to achieve, so a litter of kittens may have one "show quality" kitten – perceived as having a higher value and sold at a higher price, while the rest of the litter is relegated to "pet quality" status and might be sold to a consumer at a lower price. Unfortunately, this means that to get the single prized kitten, several others are born into a world already saturated with homeless cats, taking potential homes from those unfortunate felines.

An additional ethical concern occurs in the change of the physical makeup of a show-quality animal over time versus one that has bred naturally. For many generations, people have been selectively breeding cats to emphasize specific qualities judged in the cat show world to make them more valuable on the circuit. These traits become more and more pronounced to represent their breed as "ideal."

However, this genetic manipulation can have dire consequences to the animals as their bodies become less natural. For example, with their trademark flattened muzzles, Persian cats often have problems with breathing and eye discharge due to unnatural changes in the physical makeup in the facial structure that has become the accepted standard for the breed.

People have manipulated their breeding and mutations throughout generations of cats. This is just a single example, but there are many others.

Shelters and Rescues

Tip #17: By far, the most ethical and least risky source for your new cat is a shelter or accredited rescue.

In order to obtain funding from charitable sources, private rescues and shelters must become 501c3 certified as humane organizations, making them more reputable than other sources by default due to their need to maintain their non-profit status. Others, like county animal shelters, are regulated by state and local governments.

Shelters and rescues often work together to promote causes such as widespread spay and neuter events and adoption events to maximize the number of animals they can save within a community and reduce homeless animal populations. When rescues and no-kill shelters find that they have space to accommodate more animals, they will often "pull" at-risk animals out of the kill shelters, saving their lives, providing for their medical needs, and helping them become more attractive potential adopters.

While there is usually an adoption fee, it is generally a significantly lower cost than buying a cat from a store or a breeder. The adoption fee helps to defray the costs to the rescue or shelter of having cared for the cat. In most cases, these organizations will have already taken care of spay or neuter surgeries, an initial health exam, testing for some diseases common to cats, and at least the first round of vaccines.

As animals sometimes arrive at shelters and rescues with medical needs, some medical treatments may also have been administered. The flat adoption fee you pay for all this health care is actually a bargain. That's to say nothing of their cost of feeding and housing the cat, which can be significant if she has been in the shelter or rescue system for a while.

You may be surprised at the perks that come from adopting a cat from a shelter or rescue. Firstly, the sheer variety of available cats increases the likelihood of finding the perfect match for you. Rescues and shelters have a plethora of cats of all ages, sizes, shapes, colors, personalities, and backgrounds.

They may have been rescued from the street, they may have once been a cherished companion to a person who passed away, or they may have been surrendered to the shelter for any number of reasons. They all have stories, and they all have their love to share. The shelter staff or rescue volunteers can help you find your new best friend based on your preferences.

Breed-specific Rescues

If you are in search of a certain kind of cat, a breed-specific rescue might be just the right thing for you. A quick internet search will turn up rescues for all different breeds of cats, although some are rare enough that you may need to get on a waiting list, or the rescue may not be nearby. In these cases, interstate adoptions can sometimes be arranged, but rescue organizations all have different rules they follow, so it may be more challenging if they are far away.

Who Should You Bring Home?

A Great Matchup

The number one consideration for the good of all when choosing your new feline family member should be to match the cat to the household and vice-versa.

Tip #18: Take an honest assessment of the qualities of your household to help you make the best match.

Is your home environment busy, loud, and energetic? If so, a lively kitten or young adult cat that needs a lot of stimulation and playtime might be a good fit for your home. On the other hand, if your household is quiet and has a lower energy vibe, your high-spirited young cat will be prone to boredom and have extra energy built up that will need to be released. Such a condition can lead to behavioral issues such as destructive habits and seemingly unprovoked attacks on other household members as the cat seeks to relieve the tedium in his environment.

On the other end of the spectrum, a shy, quiet, older cat who primarily desires to lounge in a sunny spot by the window would be unhappy and stressed out in an active or chaotic home environment. Her behavior would reflect that stress in any number of ways, from continual hiding to outward displays of insecurity, such as eliminating outside her litter box. Ideally, a cat like this, with a low-key personality, would do well in a quieter, slower-paced home where she could curl up for long naps in a warm lap.

So how can you determine personality when you have a variety of choices? One of the benefits of adopting a cat from a shelter or rescue is tapping into the familiarity the shelter staff or rescue volunteers have with the individuals in their care.

The people who see and work with the cats every day can help point you in the right direction when you give them an idea of the kind of cat you are seeking. They have the inside scoop into the personality, quirks, health, history, and background of all the cats, and as feline lovers, they will do their best to help you find the perfect match.

One caveat involving cats living in a shelter environment is that sometimes cats will behave differently in a shelter than in a home. It is especially prevalent in older cats, as time in the shelter can break down their personalities, causing mental health conditions such as depression. You may find that a cat that is quiet and shy in the shelter will blossom into a cat with a big personality once he feels secure in a home environment.

Foster Failure

One very appealing feature of many shelters and rescues is their foster system. Similar to fostering human children, a feline foster agrees to take care of a cat temporarily until either the cat is adopted or the foster is unable or unwilling to continue fostering. By its very nature, foster care is a temporary housing situation. In many cases, it serves as a trial run prior to the full commitment of adoption.

Anyone who has participated in animal rescue is familiar with the term "foster failure." It is what they call it when a foster parent falls head over heels in love with the cat in their temporary care and chooses to make the situation permanent by adopting the cat outright. Many a cat has earned his spot in a loving family through foster failure.

Tip #19: Becoming a foster cat parent is an excellent option if you still have questions about adopting a particular cat or becoming a permanent cat parent.

You can approach fostering as a temporary trial run. You provide the home life for the kitty, and the rescue picks up the tab for major expenses while the cat is in your care as a foster.

Understand that the ultimate goal is for the cat to be adopted into a loving home, so if you take too long to decide, the rescue may find an adoptive home for him in the meantime. If the foster care option appeals to you, talk to a local cat rescue organization about volunteering as a cat foster parent.

How Should You Prepare for Your New Arrival?

Tip #20: Before you bring home your new cat or kitten, you should physically prepare your home.

Cats become stressed with changes to their routine and environment, and the more you can ease her transition, the better. Good preparation is the key to a smooth transition for a kitty. She will need a place all her own for a little while to help her feel safe and secure.

Safe Space

Prepare a dedicated space, preferably with places the kitty can hide until she feels comfortable to explore, in a quiet portion of the house. Some cats will set about the task of exploring right away when they come to a new place, but others need to feel secure before venturing out. Either way, give your new cat a safe space all her own, separate from other animals or humans, to serve as a familiar "retreat" for the times she might feel overwhelmed by her new situation.

Supplies – For Transport

Before you bring your new cat into your space, it is a good idea to have supplies on hand to help ease the transition. First, you will need a carrier for bringing him home. Some shelters will provide a cardboard carrier for this purpose, but it is a good idea to have one of your own already.

They come in various shapes, sizes, and materials. Find a carrier that is airline approved (in case you would like to travel with your cat someday) and that offers comfort, security, and good ventilation. A carrier like this, which opens both on the top and side, can be handy and is generally easier to manage when a cat resists being put inside.

Most cats do not organically enjoy being placed into a carrier, but a good technique for getting your new friend safely inside his transport carrier for the first time is to put him in backside first from the top. If you have a carrier that only opens on the side, tipping it up, so the entry is on the top is usually easiest.

Trying to put him in face-first will generally meet with resistance from the front legs. The quicker and more matter-of-fact you can be with the process, the less stressful it will be for both of you.

Tip #21: Consider first lining the new carrier with an unlaundered t-shirt or towel that contains your scent so that when your new friend is inside the carrier, his scent will mix with yours.

You can also try spraying this cloth liner with a pheromone spray such as Feliway to help the kitty feel secure during the transition period. Pheromone sprays and plug-ins can help cats adjust to stressful circumstances as the aroma gives them a sense of security.

The scent is essential in helping cats feel safe, so after the towel or shirt has absorbed the combination of scents, place it in the safe space you have prepared for your feline buddy. This familiar "scent cocktail" can go a long way toward building your cat's confidence in his new home.

Supplies - For Feeding

Your new feline friend may or may not be ready to eat immediately on introduction to her new environment, but it's a good idea to have feeding and watering supplies ready when she comes home.

Tip #22: The kind of bowls or bowl systems you provide for your cat can make a difference to her health and wellbeing.

Cats are prone to developing chin acne. The acne presents similarly to how it does in humans, in small, itchy bumps on the skin. To help prevent acne, consider avoiding plastic bowls, which tend to remain greasier than their glass, metal, or ceramic counterparts and contribute to the affliction.

Cat whiskers are very sensitive and can become overstimulated when they rub on the sides of your cat's bowl during mealtimes. This condition, called "whisker fatigue" or "whisker stress," is very uncomfortable for cats. To help resolve this issue, you will do your cat a big favor by providing a broad, relatively shallow bowl, so his whiskers do not touch on the sides.

When bothered by whisker fatigue, some cats will take matters literally into their own paws, pawing their food out of the food bowl and onto the floor before eating it. You can make things easier for them by simply providing a bowl that does not irritate their sensitive whisker hairs, also known as vibrissae.

Another consideration is head and neck position while eating and drinking. Placing bowls directly on the floor or other eating surfaces requires a cat to crane her neck downward to eat and can sometimes lead to vomiting. To help alleviate discomfort from this positioning, you might consider using an elevated bowl system to keep her head and neck in a more natural position while eating and drinking.

Finally, a fun and enriching feeding option involves incorporating puzzle feeders to help stimulate your cat's natural hunting and foraging instincts. Once your cat figures out how a puzzle works, the novelty wears off, so you might want to have several kinds on hand to rotate them and keep things more interesting for your kitty.

Supplies – For Watering

Tip #23: Cats need to remain well-hydrated, as they are more prone to kidney disease and urinary tract infections than many other animals, especially as they age.

Staying well-hydrated helps their kidneys flush out impurities. Therefore we want to encourage them to drink water.

Some cats drink fine from a regular water bowl, but many prefer running water. Scientists believe this preference stems from their wild ancestry, as running water tends to be safer in nature than water that is still and stagnant. In addition, cats instinctually recognize the value of drinking clean water over potentially infected water.

When given a choice, most cats will choose water from a cat fountain over water from a plain bowl of still water. To encourage plenty of water consumption, you might consider offering both a cat fountain and a water bowl, at least until you find out which your cat prefers to use.

Tip #24: The water you offer your cat should always be fresh and the receptacles clean.

Remember to change the water daily and wipe any residue from the water bowl, as slime accumulates quickly on bowl surfaces if you don't wipe it out regularly. Cat fountains need cleaning less frequently since the water is constantly moving and the fountains have filtration. Be sure, however, to change the filters with regularity and clean at least every week or two thoroughly.

Supplies – For Waste Elimination

Most cats understand how to use a litter box without any real formal training. In the wild, they naturally and instinctively deposit their waste around the perimeter of their territory to ward off rivals and predators.

Tip #25: It's important to provide a suitable litter box – or ideally, more than one – to help keep waste where you want it, rather than dealing with the cat putting it where you don't want it.

The box itself should be large enough for the kitty to move around within it comfortably. He will want space to move around and scratch the substrate (aka "cat litter") inside it without feeling cramped or claustrophobic.

Because the process of waste elimination makes cats feel vulnerable to attack from predators, the safer you help him feel during the experience, the less likely he is to do his business outside the litter box. Although people often prefer a litter box with a cover, cats usually feel differently.

A covered litter box blocks their vision of anyone or anything coming near from any direction other than the hole where they enter the box. Placing the litter box strategically in an out-of-the-way corner can have the same effect if the cat's view is obscured at all.

Cats prefer to feel safe, and anything that blocks their vision of the world around them while they are in the vulnerable position of eliminating can make them feel insecure. Therefore, litter box insecurity could potentially lead to their discharging elsewhere but in the box.

By the same token, if the box is placed in a chaotic area with a lot of noise and/or activity going on, the cat might feel overwhelmed and afraid. So, again, the best bet is a nice neutral location that gives the cat a clear line of vision and an easy escape route from multiple directions.

In addition to litter boxes, you will need to provide some substrate, or kitty litter, to fill the box, and have a litter scooper for cleanup. There are many different kinds of litter on the market.

Tip #26: Take cues from your cat regarding her preferred litter type. Some experimentation may be necessary at the beginning.

Litters are made from all kinds of substances. Some include clay, silica, walnut, newspaper made into pellets, wheat, pine, and corn. Naturally, they have different qualities, and it may take some trial and error to figure out what kind you and your cat like and agree upon.

Some cats have a preference, and others do not. Cats may have a pronounced inclination for one kind over another based on the texture under their paws and/or the smell. Keep in mind that a cat's sense of smell is much stronger than that of a human, so cat litters with a strong scent can be overwhelming for them.

Most cats will prefer an unscented litter over one with a strong chemical smell, and simply keeping the box clean will help you manage the odor better than using a strongly scented cat litter, which usually doesn't really keep the cat waste smell away so much as it mixes in another strong odor along with it.

Supplies – For Sleepy-Time

Tip #27: Cats spend a significant portion of their time sleeping, so having comfortable and secure places to nap is essential.

Most cats will not settle for just a single bed, and some will reject every expensive bed you offer them, opting instead to curl up in a box you left lying around. Others enjoy the finer things in life and will love that expensive marshmallow bed you provide them. Or they will want to stretch out in a sunbeam on your hardwood floor.

Until you know the cat, it is hard to guess what kind of sleeper he will be, but it is up to you to provide different types of comfy places in his safe space for him to try, especially at first. You don't necessarily need to spend a great deal of money on an expensive cat bed if, for example, your kitty's safe space contains human furniture so he can curl up for a nap on the bed or sofa.

However, he may not feel secure sleeping out in the open, especially when he first comes into your home, so if you can provide a comfy box lined with something soft, perhaps in an out-of-the-open spot like a closet, he might appreciate your thoughtful gesture. But, again, the key is giving him multiple kinds of options.

Supplies – For Playtime and Interaction

Tip #28: One of the best ways for you to bond with your cat is through regular playtime together.

Predatory creatures that they are, cats simulate the hunt through playtime. We will delve deeper into this topic later. For now, though, while you are preparing the kitty's safe space for her arrival, have some toys available for the essential activity of playtime.

Once again, cats are all different, and their preferences are as varied as their coat colors. Therefore, it's a good idea to have some independent play toys like small, lightweight balls and catnip mice for your cat to play with while you are unavailable.

It's just as important – perhaps even more so – for you to have interactive toys like wand toys that you can use to replicate prey movements to activate your cat's predatory drive. Again, this is usually the most beneficial kind of play for most cats.

In terms of types of toys, there will likely be a lot of toys you buy for your cat that she completely ignores, and then she'll surprise you by having a wild play session with something completely unexpected, like a lid from a pen or some other silly object. It may be difficult to predict what kinds of things turn on your own cat's predatory drive until you know her a little bit better, but since play is vital for her wellbeing, it's a good idea to have a few different kinds of toys ready for when she moves in. Fortunately, most cat toys are not too outrageously priced, so the learning process doesn't have to cost you too much.

Chapter 1 Review

- Your decision to become a feline guardian is a good one for both you and the cat (or cats!). Sharing your home with a cat brings mental and physical health benefits and gives a loving home to a cat that might otherwise remain homeless or even be killed for the misfortune of having no one else to love him.
- Before committing to bringing home a new feline roommate, be sure to do your research, consider all angles, and prepare to care for her throughout her entire lifetime.
- Important considerations before jumping into a commitment to a cat, look to the future and include finances, housing, family planning, and lifestyle. Even potential allergic reactions can come into play down the line.
- Sourcing your new friend can carry both practical and ethical ramifications. The ideal choice is to adopt from a reputable shelter or rescue organization.
- Rather than choosing your cat based on physical appearance alone, it is best to find a perfect match for your household based on personality and connection. Sometimes the cat will choose you. Be open to that! Sometimes the cat will know best!
- To ensure a smooth transition to your home, you should prepare with a quiet, safe space and all the essential supplies before bringing home your new family member.

Chapter 2: Let's Get to the Vet!

It's a great idea to take your new kitty to the veterinarian as soon as possible. In fact, it doesn't hurt to have an appointment scheduled to occur before you even take him home.

A thorough initial examination serves multiple purposes: it establishes a positive relationship with your veterinarian at the earliest opportunity, and it helps to ensure that your new friend is not introducing any undesirable parasites or pathogens to your home that he may have picked up in his previous home. Of course, it also helps to reassure you that your kitty is in tip-top shape and/or alerts you to any potential issues.

With the availability of infinite online information and resources at our fingertips these days, you may be tempted to consult "Dr. Google" before or as an alternative to taking your cat to visit a vet. While it does not hurt to use your available means, your veterinarian and/or holistic medical provider should be your first source of information and resources.

Remember that although there is a lot of great information on the Internet, there is as much or more misinformation. Your cat's health care team can help you determine what is valuable and what is best ignored. Consider the web a supplement, not a primary source.

Choosing the Best Vet for You and Your Cat

Tip #29: Establish a Health Care Team You Can Trust

Various factors go into your veterinary choices, and only you truly know which values hold the greatest weight for you. Some elements to consider include: location, price structures, areas of expertise, credentials, facility, and staff. It's not necessary to talk much about price structures or location here. You will determine for yourself what is acceptable to you for those considerations, and my advice would be redundant.

Areas of Expertise or Certification

Some veterinarians do not have any particular areas of expertise or specialty, which is fine if you immediately connect with your new kitty's health care team. However, the ideal situation would be to find a "Cat Friendly" and "Fear-Free" certified feline specialist who is at least open-minded about, if not a practitioner of, integrative medicine. Your cat will then be in the best possible hands, covering all the essential bases.

AAHA Accreditation

Not all veterinary hospitals or clinics are certified through the American Animal Hospital Association (AAHA). To get this accreditation, they need to pass evaluations in a full range of veterinary skills and practices related to animal patient care.

The accreditation covers entire medical hospitals or clinics. It must be kept up to date regularly to maintain the certification, so it is not simply a matter of passing one time to earn the honor of displaying an AAHA certificate. Instead, it ensures medical staff continues to maintain the most up-to-date best practices.

Feline Specialists

Some communities have feline-only practices available. A feline-only practice has the benefit of a less stressful visit to the veterinarian as no loud barking dogs will snuffle at your cat's carrier while she waits in the lobby. Also, the practice will cater to the unique needs of felines and have a generally calmer, more relaxing atmosphere.

A vet specializing in cats will have more dedicated expertise in handling your cat and diagnosing ailments common to the feline persuasion. In addition, cats are highly prone to stress, especially when taken out of their regular environment and put into new circumstances. Stress, fear, and anxiety comprise the most common feline disorders and can be significantly minimized. Therefore, a veterinarian who can help mitigate feline stress is a valuable asset.

"Fear-Free" Certified

A valuable certification to seek in a health care team is "Fear-Free" accreditation. This endorsement has been available to veterinary professionals since 2016. The certification coursework is available and tailored to various animal care professionals, including veterinary staff, trainers, groomers, shelter personnel, and, very recently, sitters. The organization even provides educational materials suitable for animal guardians through their "Fear-Free Happy Homes" program.

Tip #30: Consider joining the "Fear-Free Happy Homes" movement.

The curriculum was developed by medical care professionals of varying specialties, including veterinary behaviorists, pain specialists, internal medicine specialists, and veterinarians within the shelter environment. Additionally, non-medical experts in animal care, such as trainers and groomers, assisted with creating the coursework.

The "Fear-Free" program focuses on minimizing stress, fear, and anxiety in companion animals while simultaneously encouraging emotional well-being through enrichment. Finding professionals who understand how to reduce anxiety for your feline friend in otherwise potentially stressful situations will prove incredibly valuable for your kitty's welfare.

"Cat Friendly" Certified

Because cats come with a unique set of challenges compared with other species, the American Association of Feline Practitioners (AAFP) recently began offering a certification program designed with feline needs in mind. The "Cat Friendly" program has been available since 2020. It is quickly gaining traction among veterinarians – especially those dedicated to addressing the special needs of their feline patients to reduce the stress commonly associated with traditional veterinary care.

As it is a curriculum on the cutting edge of feline veterinary medicine, many practitioners have not yet had the opportunity to complete this certification. They are not remiss if they do not have it. However, it would be desirable if your new kitty's veterinary team prioritizes cats in their practice and makes an effort to earn the accreditation.

You may be surprised to learn how many Cat-Friendly certified practitioners have already completed certification in your area. In this book's "Resources" section, you can find the web address to help you locate a team near you.

Tip #31: Visit the "Cat Friendly" website to stay informed with feline content.

An added bonus to the Cat-Friendly website is the wealth of information offered there for cat guardians. Not only can you find the best veterinarians, but you can also consult the site as a trustworthy source of information on various feline health and behavior subjects. You can even sign up for a newsletter that will provide you with the most current information on all things cat-related.

Integrative Care

Further, a veterinarian who either practices integrative medicine outright or is open-minded to your taking a collaborative approach and consulting multiple care providers will help to ensure your cat has the most balanced and well-rounded health care.

Tip #32: Consider using a holistic and balanced approach to your cat's wellness care.

An integrative medical approach considers the entire range of experiences and represents a blend of traditional and holistic medical disciplines. It means treatment addresses more than just symptoms of disease but considers the cat's body, mind, and spirit to support total well-being and health.

The veterinarians in your cat's circle of experience might be a general practitioner (ideally, one who specializes in feline health), a holistic practitioner, and potentially, an emergency veterinary team for the times your primary health practitioners are unavailable.

Preparing ahead to find these resources can be very valuable if and when the need for emergency care arises. When every minute counts, you will be glad you had the foresight to plan ahead.

Think of yourself, since you are your cat's primary advocate and decision-maker, as a crucial part – indeed, as the leader of – your cat's healthcare team. So ask the hard questions and advocate when necessary for your cat's well-being.

Facility: Clean and Calm

Tip #33: Heed your senses and instincts regarding the suitability of a veterinary facility for you and your cat.

In terms of the facility, it doesn't matter much if the building itself is on the older side, but it should be well-maintained and clean. Let your gut and your senses guide you. Can you smell animal urine? With their heightened sense of smell, cats can smell much more than you can, which adds stress to the experience of being at the veterinary clinic if a previous patient has left his mark and the odor is still present.

Do you see messes? Is there a lot of loud noise and chaos? These can all be indicators that the facility might not be the best choice for you and your cat.

Like a hospital for people, potential infectious disease walking into the facility at any time can pose a risk to human and non-human animals alike. For example, if the staff fails to clean up messes promptly, your cat could be exposed to contaminants that might make him sick.

Some veterinary clinics have a separate entrance for animals experiencing potentially contagious symptoms to help reduce the spread of disease within the hospital setting. That is a good sign that the facility takes proper precautions to keep you and your cat safe. It is not essential but is definitely a great system that indicates forward-thinking on the part of the practice.

Support Staff: Professional, Friendly, and Motivated

Tip #34: Watch for obvious red flags with the health care support staff.

The support staff is the backbone of the veterinary hospital, and their behavior reflects how well the team runs. You want to see staff members who have confidence in their respective roles, who behave professionally, and who appear happy to have you and your cat in their workspace.

If the energy feels frenetic or lackluster in the veterinary office, that might indicate the hospital is understaffed or lacks competence. These are red flags, possibly meaning the staff may be unable to give proper care to each patient, might be prone to poor medical record-keeping, or might provide minimal priority to their patients.

Of course, you should understand that in veterinary medicine, just like in human medicine, sometimes true emergencies occur, which can temporarily bring craziness with them. So be vigilant, but be fair, too.

Procedures and Recommendations to Expect

Basic Exam and Bloodwork

Now that you have your new cat in the vet clinic, what procedures can you expect? In most cases, for an initial visit, the veterinarian will want to conduct a thorough examination. It will include checking your kitty's vital signs such as temperature and pulse. In addition, the veterinarian will likely check the external systems, looking into his ears and eyes, checking his mouth, teeth, and gums, feeling for abnormalities along his entire body, and checking for external parasites on the skin.

To be especially thorough at the first visit, they may suggest you allow them to take a small blood sample to help them establish a "baseline" or to ascertain your cat's version of normal numbers associated with internal organ functioning.

Tip #35: Allowing the veterinarian to assess your cat's bloodwork can give you an early baseline or early intervention for underlying issues.

Running bloodwork helps them determine organ health and will be helpful down the road if and when your cat becomes ill so that they can compare your kitty's regular readings with her readings when sick. Bloodwork on the initial exam is not necessarily standard, especially because many people balk at the extra expense of lab work. Still, it is a thorough approach to your cat's health care, so it is not abnormal either.

Common Recommendations – Sterilization

Tip #36: If your cat is intact, have them spayed or neutered as soon as they are old enough, according to your veterinarian's suggestion.

If your cat is not yet spayed or neutered, your veterinarian will likely want to schedule this surgery as soon as possible, or – if your kitty is still very young – as soon as she is old enough. Veterinarians recommend sexual sterilization for several important reasons outlined below.

Spaying Your Female Cat

First, having your female cat spayed prevents later medical issues related to sex hormones. The most common conditions in this category are mammary tumors and the severe uterine infection known as pyometra, which can be deadly and expensive to treat.

Secondly, sterilizing her prevents her heat cycle. A female cat in heat can attract every intact male within a mile radius, so you might find new cats hanging around the outside of your home, hoping for a chance to breed with her.

The hormonal urgency she experiences brings with it the risk that she will try to escape outside to meet up with the male cats. A cat in heat can be wily and persistent, so her safety is at risk when she hits her estrus.

Thirdly, her behavior while in heat will become challenging for anyone who shares space with her. She will howl incessantly. She may become unusually affectionate and rub herself on everything in her environment.

She will likely spend an unusual amount of time licking her private parts – which become not so private, as she displays them quite prominently to the world at large and they may even become swollen. To telegraph her condition to the neighborhood tomcats, she may spray urine on vertical surfaces. None of these behaviors make for a pleasant roommate!

Neutering Your Male Cat

You may be thinking at this point that it is better to have a male cat so you won't have to deal with all the nonsense associated with the female hormones. Think again. If you choose not to neuter your male cat, you will still have serious issues with which to contend; in fact, perhaps even more so.

First, male cats are also prone to medical issues related to sex hormones. Removing their testicles eliminates the possibility of testicular cancer and enlarged prostate. It may also make them less susceptible to an inflammation of the perineum and anus called a perineal fistula, which presents similarly to hemorrhoids.

Secondly, an intact male cat can be relentless in its pursuit of a female in heat. As he can smell her estrus from as far as a mile away, he will do everything in his power to escape the confines of his home to find her. His ingenuity to escape may surprise you!

In his quest to breed, he becomes less aware of his surroundings, making him exceptionally vulnerable to predators and car collisions. In addition, his instinct to fight with rival toms will multiply significantly, which is another health and safety risk.

Finally, male cats are extraordinarily territorial in nature and highly prone to marking their territorial boundaries. They do this primarily through urine marking and will soak their environment with urine to keep rivals away. An added "bonus" is the enhanced pungency of the odor of intact male urine, which is stronger than that of females or neutered males. It's incredibly stinky!

Common Recommendations – Vaccinations

Tip #37: After discussing factors such as your cat's age and projected lifestyle with your veterinary team, follow their advice regarding the proposed vaccine schedule and keep your cat current on the vaccinations as recommended.

At the initial visit, your veterinarian will want to know which – if any – vaccines your cat has already had. You may have received a record of vaccines at the point of adoption. However, if you procured your new friend from a less reliable source, it's they may have told you some version of, "she is up to date on all of her shots."

Tip #38: Try to obtain records of specific vaccines your cat received prior to your adopting her, complete with the dates she received them.

Unfortunately, the vague term "up-to-date" really is useless without the details. You will need a written record of which vaccines she received, the date on which she received them, and the schedule and number of each vaccine she received.

The first time a cat receives the standard cat vaccines, she will need a "booster" a few weeks later to ensure full protection. Kittens need additional boosters. In the absence of accurate information, your vet will need to start at the beginning of the cat's vaccination schedule regardless of the claim someone made to you that she is "up-to-date."

Tip #39: Avoid exposing your new family member to other cats before completing the initial vaccine series.

Remember that your cat or kitten may be vulnerable to disease before receiving the complete series of vaccinations. Try to avoid both direct and indirect exposure (for example, pathogens you may bring home on your hands or clothing from a sick cat) as much as possible before finishing the vaccine series. Some pathogens can live for long periods in the environment.

To obtain a license for your cat with your local municipality, you will need to provide a rabies vaccine certificate as proof that your cat has received the vaccine. If you did not receive the certificate at the time of adoption or purchase, your veterinarian would need to give the vaccine again to provide you with the necessary documentation.

After the initial round of vaccines, your cat may only need them annually or even every several years, depending on various factors that her doctor will determine from discussion with you. Such considerations are primarily lifestyle-based and take risk factors into account.

Common Recommendations - Parasite Control and Elimination

External Parasites: Fleas, Ticks, Mites

Fleas and Ticks

The veterinarian's examination will include checking for obvious signs of external parasites such as fleas, ticks, and mites. For example, to detect fleas, the vet will usually use a flea comb in various areas around your cat's skin to check for flea dirt, the waste product of fleas, which indicates fleas are present.

Tip #40: Keep a flea comb on hand at home so you can check your cat regularly for fleas and flea dirt. Regularly flea combing your cat can also help you locate ticks for early intervention.

Visual and tactile cues help the veterinarian find ticks, as an engorged tick can be as large as a pencil eraser. A thorough examination with both eyes and hands, especially for someone familiar with ticks, can find them easily.

Mites

Ear mites may be a bit trickier to detect, as they are technically external parasites, but they live within the ear canal and are barely visible to the naked eye. The vet will use a lighted otoscope to look down into the depths of the ear canal for signs of mites, such as tissue redness, irritation, and mite waste. Then, they will likely take a swab sample of the ear discharge and view it under a microscope for a definitive diagnosis.

Tip #41: Watch your kitty for signs of discomfort around the ears, such as pawing at them excessively, frequent head-shaking, or holding each ear at a radically different angle. Do not ignore the signs of potential ear infestation or infection. Schedule a veterinary visit pronto!

Internal Parasites: Intestinal Parasites and Heartworm

Intestinal Parasites

Intestinal parasites are relatively common in cats. In some cases, kittens are even born with them, having had the intruders pass from mother cat to kitten. Most intestinal parasites require a stool sample to diagnose. If you have a fresh specimen, you should bring it with you to the veterinary appointment so the staff can look at a smear of it under a microscope to check for the presence of intestinal worms or protozoan parasites.

Tip #42: Bring a fresh stool sample to your veterinarian for each wellness visit to check for intestinal parasites. It is okay if the specimen has cat litter stuck to it.

The diagnostic exception to the rule is tapeworms. Examining a stool sample under a microscope is less likely to reveal the presence of a tapeworm. Still, tapeworm segments are significantly easier to see with the naked eye, as they usually present as ribbon-like, flat, white things hanging around the cat's rectum or like sesame seeds if already dried in the stool. They are about the length of a grain of rice while still fresh.

Adding to the disgust factor, they may even be moving when you see them. Cats pick up tapeworm when they groom themselves and inadvertently ingest an infected flea, increasing the importance of flea control to prevent not just the fleas but also the tapeworm. As with other intestinal parasites, the veterinarian can prescribe medications to eliminate them.

If you suspect that your cat has intestinal parasites, bring a stool sample to the clinic to diagnose the kind of parasite rather than finding a random deworming medication at the pet supply store or using leftover medications prescribed to a friend's cat. Veterinarians prescribe different medicines for different varieties of parasites.

Heartworm

People generally associate heartworms more with dogs than with cats, but it is possible for cats to be infected too. Heartworms are transmitted through mosquitoes, so even indoor kitties may be affected, especially in regions of the country where infected mosquitoes most readily reside. Although cats tend to resist heartworms better than dogs, heartworm infection can be more devastating and deadly for a cat once contracted.

Veterinarians usually use a combination of diagnostics to detect heartworm in cats, prompted by recognizing the more common clinical signs. However, the symptoms that might indicate heartworm are also commonly associated with myriad other ailments, making heartworms particularly difficult to identify without conducting multiple kinds of tests. Therefore, it would be unusual for your vet to diagnose heartworms on an initial exam unless you report multiple symptoms that inspire them to run such tests.

Treatments and Preventatives for Parasites

Following thorough examination, your kitty's vet will prescribe medications to treat any parasites detected and will likely suggest prophylactic treatments to prevent future parasitic infestations. The most common of these will guard against fleas and ticks, although in some areas where heartworms are common, they may recommend a heartworm preventative as well.

Tip #43: Only give your cat medication that has been prescribed to them for a particular condition, and follow the instructions on the label.

Ignoring parasitic prevention can spell disaster for your kitty, so please follow veterinary recommendations. Avoid over-the-counter flea preparations containing pyrethrums or permethrins, including flea collars. Over time, fleas have developed resistance to these substances, so they are less effective than the solutions your vet will suggest.

More importantly, these chemicals are toxic to cats, and the companies marketing them behave irresponsibly in selling them for use on cats. Overexposure to them can be fatal, as I witnessed firsthand during my employment in the veterinary industry.

Ticks are less common to cats than they are to dogs. It may partly be because cats groom themselves so frequently and so thoroughly that they may groom them off before they have a chance to attach fully. However, tick-borne diseases like Lyme disease can cause significant illness leading to death in cats if not treated quickly, so it is best to prevent ticks from biting your cat in the first place.

Common Recommendations - Microchip Insertion

Tip #44: Microchip identification is essential even if your cat wears an identification tag or has an identifying tattoo.

Unless your cat previously received a microchip in his former home, rescue, or shelter, your veterinarian will likely suggest having one inserted during the initial visit. In the context of domestic animals, a microchip is a small piece of technology about the size of a rice grain, which is inserted below the surface of your kitty's skin, using a sharp instrument specifically designed to do so.

The implanted piece does not provide any tracking mechanism and sits below the skin's surface, ready for a scanner to read the unique alphanumeric code associated with your cat. In the event you and your cat become separated – for example, if she dashes out the door unexpectedly, breaks through a window screen to get to a bird outside the window, or gets lost in the chaos surrounding some unforeseen disaster – any shelter or veterinarian encountering her can use a universal scanner to reveal her code, which will trace back to you.

All microchip numbers are stored on a universal database associated with the person's contact information most recently registered to the unique alphanumeric code on the cat's microchip. Thus, in theory, any universal scanner should lead to a reunion between the cat and human associated with the code.

Tip #45: Be sure your information on file with the microchip company remains current at all times.

Without correct information in the database, no one can find you, so be sure to keep your contact information up-to-date with the microchip registry company. Having a microchip with current registration information can be the puzzle piece that reunites you with your cat in the event of unanticipated separation.

Alternative Forms of Identification

Tattoos

In lieu of microchips, some cats have tattoos as a form of permanent identification. However, this is a less foolproof method of ensuring you and your cat can be reunited following a separation, as tattoos can fade and become difficult to read properly.

Additionally, there is no universal tattoo database, so tracing a cat based on a tattoo can prove problematic. Therefore, even if your cat has an identifying tattoo, she should also have a microchip as an added precaution.

Collars and ID Tags

Your cat may wear a collar and identification tag with your contact information, and that is a good idea so that if he somehow finds himself lost outside, his finder can easily contact you. The problem is that such accessories can fall off or be purposely removed.

Firstly, collars without a breakaway feature can get caught on things and strangle or otherwise injure your cat, so any collar your cat wears should be a breakaway collar as a safety precaution. If the collar does get caught on something, it could pull off, leaving the kitty naked, with no collar and no tag at all.

Secondly, tags can break off or get damaged, rendering the information on them difficult or impossible to read. Collars and tags, while helpful, do not represent a permanent form of identification.

Thirdly, someone who finds your kitty and wants to keep him can easily remove a collar and claim the right to keep your cat. Under such circumstances, a microchip provides proof that your cat really is your cat.

Chapter 2 Review:

- Choosing the right veterinarian for you and your cat is an important decision. Areas of expertise, accreditation, facility, and support staff all represent critical factors to consider when making your choice.
- Among the most imperative items to address for the health of your cat is sexual sterilization. For both males and females, these alterations will prevent serious health and behavioral concerns in the future. They additionally help to address the overpopulation and consequential death of countless cats within your community.
- Vaccinating your cat against common feline diseases is essential for maintaining health. However, vaccination schedules may vary, depending on various lifestyle differences. Your veterinarian can help you to choose the best plan for your kitty's individual circumstances.
- A vital part of your cat's visit to the veterinarian involves both internal and external parasites. If veterinary staff find evidence of parasites, they will prescribe treatment. However, even if they do not detect any parasites, they will likely recommend or prescribe preventatives, which are essential to maintaining a healthy kitty.
- If your cat does not already have a microchip implanted under the skin, having your vet perform the service is the best way to ensure you will be reunited with the kitty in the event of unforeseen separation. The procedure is quick and safe. Just be sure to keep your information updated with the microchip manufacturer's database.

Chapter 3: Healthful Living

Feline Nutrition

Nutrition is the most fundamental building block for physical health. The same thing holds true for every animal body, from one belonging to a fruit fly or blue whale to that of a human being. Of course, your cat is no exception.

Tip #46: Providing a balanced, nutritionally complete, and biologically appropriate diet throughout her lifetime is the worthiest and most effective way to support your cat's soundest health and longevity.

Feeding her a nutrient-dense, species-appropriate diet is paramount to maintaining her health from the inside out. The terms "biologically appropriate" and "species-appropriate" refer to dietary formulations that are nearest to what a cat might consume in her natural environment. In contrast, traditional cat foods were created in lab settings with profits a higher priority than the nutrition intended with the feline body in mind.

We have only been purchasing food for our cats for less than a century. In the grand scheme of our relationship with them, that is a relatively short time. Prior to that, they functioned mainly as pest control for humans, ingesting the prey that their bodies are designed to process.

As our relationship with our feline friends evolved, we began allowing them into our homes and eventually sharing our homes with them full time. As most people prefer not to share homes with common feline prey such as rodents, small reptiles, and insects, and with the proliferation of "pest control" services, the increasing issue of cat confinement brought about a necessity for humans to provide substitute nourishment for the cats in their homes.

Special Dietary Needs

Tip #47: Accommodate your cat's special dietary requirements.

Cats have unique dietary needs and will become very unhealthy if those needs are ignored. Unlike humans, dogs, bears, and other animals, cats are obligate carnivores, meaning that their bodies require meat to be healthy. Other animals, including you or your friend's dog, can thrive and remain robust with a vegetarian diet and, in fact, will likely be healthier than carnivorous counterparts, given a well-executed approach to the vegetarian diet.

This notion does not hold true for cats. Well-meaning vegetarians who try to impose a vegetarian diet on their cats are committing a grave error in doing so. Feline bodies process nutrients differently than other species.

For example, like many other species, cats require dietary Vitamin A. Humans and dogs can absorb Vitamin A from ingesting carrots or other plants. Unfortunately, your kitty does not have that luxury, as her body cannot convert vegetable-sourced Vitamin A to use it properly. Instead, she needs animal-based fats and needs to obtain them from an animal source, such as eggs or meat.

Another example is the feline's absolute need for the amino acid taurine, which is only available from animal sources. Without adequate taurine in her diet, your kitty could experience a diverse range of symptoms like digestive problems, degeneration of the retina, which could lead to blindness if left untreated, and heart issues like cardiomyopathy or a weakening of the muscles surrounding the heart.

Taurine deficiency also leads to gestational problems and is especially problematic for queens – female cats who are pregnant or nursing. In addition, low birth weight and fetal abnormalities commonly affect kittens born to mothers with inadequate taurine consumption.

Choosing High-Quality Cat Food

Tip #48: Learn how to be savvy about reading your cat's food labels, and don't let food companies hoodwink or manipulate you with their AAFCO claims.

When reading cat food labels, you will likely notice a statement regarding feeding tests completed using AAFCO standards or procedures. Such information appears to guarantee a standard of high quality.

The American Association of Feed Control Officials (AAFCO) is an independent not-for-profit organization that sets the regulations surrounding labeling for feline diets – along with diets formulated for other species in the United States. Their job is to ensure that the label is accurate concerning the formulation.

It sounds good for a diet to be "AAFCO Approved," but that can be misleading. The word "approved" sounds like an endorsement, but in no way does it guarantee the quality of the product behind the label. In fact, AAFCO does NOT approve of any cat foods at all. Through the miracle of advertising and labeling, brands can mislead the public with the carefully worded claims they make involving AAFCO.

Alternative and Holistic Diets – Higher Quality Traditional Forms and Raw

Tip #49: Remain open-minded about alternatives to familiar ways of feeding your cat.

High-Quality Traditional Diets

You are no doubt familiar with feline diets that you may have seen at your local grocery stores, big-box animal supply chain stores, feed stores, and even your local veterinary clinic. Alternatively, you can purchase food for your cat through online retailers or local natural or holistic suppliers, some of which are now chains and some of which are more in the local-only "mom-and-pop" vein.

Generally speaking, most of your higher-quality alternative types of feline diets are more readily available through these latter means – online retailers or natural supply markets. These are diets you will find in familiar forms of packaging such as cans or pouches, but that include more meat, higher protein percentages, minimal or no grains, low carbohydrates, and lower levels of preservatives and processing than the cheaper versions you might find on your grocery store shelf.

Raw or "BARF" Diets

However, cat food is no longer available only in the traditional kibble, pouch, or canned form. Typically, feline nutritionists and holistic practitioners will recommend a diet formulated to help the cat's body best process the food. In addition, many tout the benefits of a raw diet for cats.

Alternatively referred to as a BARF diet (either "biologically appropriate raw food" OR "bones and raw food" depending who you ask), it is a raw diet that consists of uncooked bones, organ meats, and flesh. It is the closest replication of what your cat's wild ancestors and homeless cousins would eat in a natural setting. In other words, it is what your cat's body was created or evolved to consume and convert to energy.

One benefit to feeding your feline friend a raw diet is higher digestibility. That translates to his body using the nutrients better and needing to excrete less food, which also means less waste in the litter box, and the waste that does appear is generally less smelly and unappealing.

Tip #50: Avoid "junk food" for your kitty.

Additionally, raw diets are more natural and therefore have fewer processed ingredients, making them much more nutrient-dense and therefore much more healthful for your cat. Unfortunately, the processing used for most standard cat foods cooks out most of the crucial nutrients, essentially turning ingredients that would have otherwise been healthful into empty calories for kitty. In layman's terms: processing turns healthy ingredients into junk food.

Preservatives increase the junk food factor. The additives used to make foods "shelf stable" provide another source of empty calories to traditional cat foods.

Of course, the other side of that coin is one of the disadvantages of feeding your kitty a raw diet. Put simply; it can be downright inconvenient.

Tip #51: When feeding a raw diet to your cat that you need to defrost, be especially mindful to avoid bacterial growth.

One of the most common forms of raw food comes frozen, necessitating a thaw-and-serve cycle. Once the food is thawed, you must keep it in the refrigerator and serve it within the first few days.

Also, whatever kitty does not eat immediately needs to go back into the refrigerator quickly. You must throw away defrosted raw food that sits out for any length of time. Lack of preservatives may be more healthful but can open the door for bacterial overgrowth if you do not handle the food properly.

There are freeze-dried versions of raw diets that can significantly increase the shelf stability to levels that rival standard kibble. These can be rehydrated for healthier moisture content or served in their freeze-dried form if that is your cat's preference. However, if your cat only wants to eat the freeze-dried form, you should supplement his diet with nutrient-dense food with high moisture content and ensure he consumes enough water from other sources.

Tip #52: Prioritize high-quality nutrition in the short run to save on veterinary bills in the long run.

The other disadvantage you may perceive about raw diets is what appears to be a higher cost per feeding. However, when you factor in the savings on the back end – a cat with healthier bodily systems needing less veterinary intervention, the savings could be significant in the longer run.

The Do-It-Yourself Route

Also, some people choose to take a more "Do-It-Yourself" approach and make their own homemade cat foods, which can cut costs significantly over premade and pre-packaged diets available for purchase. This feeding method might come with cost savings but decreases the convenience factor quite a bit.

Tip #53: If you choose to make your cat's food rather than purchasing it premade, be sure to consult a feline nutritionist first.

Formulating your own cat food comes with some significant caveats. First of all, the diet needs to be nutritionally balanced and include the correct percentages of all the nutrients the kitty needs to maintain robust health.

You also need to be very careful to avoid introducing infectious diseases and bacteria – both for your cat and for your family, in the food preparation space in your home. Preparing homemade cat food is a venture that should ONLY be undertaken under the supervision and guidance of a knowledgeable feline nutritionist and/or holistic health practitioner.

Feline nutritionists have the real scoop on the most healthful foods to give to our cats. This topic is very critical, but the details go beyond the scope of this book, as they could fill an entire book all on their own. So instead, we'll include web addresses in the resources section for more comprehensive advice and information directly from feline nutritionists so you can research the subject and learn how to support your cat's health and fitness from the inside out.

Probiotics for Cats

Probiotics are currently a hot topic in the zeitgeist. You may be hearing about the health benefits of consuming probiotics to replenish your gut flora.

They can reduce inflammation in various parts of your body, enhance your immune system, improve or treat intestinal disorders, and replenish microflora losses incurred from taking antibiotics. You may even be taking probiotics yourself for any of these purposes.

Tip #54: Consider supplementing your kitty's diet with probiotics to promote vitality that originates within the gastrointestinal system.

Probiotics have the same benefits for felines that they have for humans. However, cats and people have very different naturally occurring microbiome flora, so probiotics designed for humans would not help cats and vice-versa. Therefore, you should only give your kitty probiotics explicitly formulated for cats.

Sometimes veterinarians prescribe probiotics to counter particular health problems, but they are generally safe for everyday use. In addition, daily supplemental probiotic use can help to keep your feline friend feeling fine.

Regardless of the safety of probiotic use, it's still a good idea to consult your kitty's veterinarian or holistic specialist before beginning any dietary supplement program. They can guide you in best practices specific to your cat and his needs.

Treats

Tip #55: Choose a variety of healthful snacks for your kitty and offer them strategically.

It's rewarding to share treats with our friends, but it's a good idea to consider the circumstances and the ramifications of doing so when giving treats to our feline friends. Then choose the treats carefully according to the situation. Some treats are healthful enough to be given regularly, and others should be reserved for truly special occasions.

For example, single-ingredient meat treats like freeze-dried salmon and freeze-dried chicken are a good choice that would be appropriate for everyday use, as they are healthful and nutritious. In addition, most cats like these snacks, and they tend to be very shelf-stable.

On the other end of the moisture spectrum, cats and their guardians alike celebrate the relatively new trend toward "lick-able" treats. Moisture-rich and meat-based, these treats that come in pouches or squeezable plastic tubes are gaining popularity. Brands like "Inaba Churu," "Fussie Cat," and "Purina Fancy Feast" offer grain-free versions, eliminating ingredients that would not occur in a typical natural feline diet.

Tip #56: Even healthful cat treats are not sufficient nutrition on their own — no matter what your cat tries to tell you. Don't let him manipulate you.

The key here is balance. Don't let your cat talk you into feeding him a diet consisting of treats only — even if they are healthful treats. His diet will become severely out of balance if he consumes only snack foods. Treats are meant to be supplemental to a well-rounded and balanced diet.

Tip #57: Consuming junk food can be okay if it's only occasional, but doing so regularly counters your nutritional goals.

High carbohydrate junk food treats full of processed ingredients and preservatives will not hurt your kitty in small quantities if you only provide them occasionally. It's equivalent to allowing yourself to eat cake and ice cream on your birthday or another special occasion when you normally stick to a healthful dietary regimen. Tip #58: Avoid giving cow's milk to your cat.

It bears noting in this section that people often mistakenly give cow's milk and its products to cats as a treat because we grew up with images of cats happily lapping up bowls or saucers of milk. It's true that many cats enjoy cow's milk and products made from cow's milk.

However, it is also true that most cats are lactose intolerant and their bodies do not handle such provisions well. The only milk feline bodies should ingest under normal circumstances is cat's milk — from their mothers when they are kittens.

***Tip #59: Save very high-value treats for behavioral
rewards.***

Try offering your cat a variety of mostly healthful treats to
determine which kinds he enjoys the most. The snacks he holds in
the highest regard can serve double-duty as bribes or as rewards for
performing desired behaviors – like taking his medication, learning
new skills during training, or submitting to a nail trim when he
would rather be hanging out in a sunbeam. Reserving those high-
value snacks only for those special times when you need to offer
extra encouragement will help you gain compliance from a hesitant
kitty.

Feline Body Condition Score

One metric your veterinary practitioners use to help determine your
cat's health is the Body Condition Score (BCS). The fundamental
locations on your kitty's body where the vet observes the amount of
fat present, the hips, waist, and ribs, serve as primary indicators of
body condition. The doctor assigns a number from one to nine
based on those observations.

Each number along the continuum represents 10% away from a
score of five, which is at the center. For example, receiving a body
condition score of four or five indicates that your feline friend is
doing well with the ideal body condition for her frame. If the doctor
scores her at a 7, she is 20% overweight, while a score of 2 would
mean she is underweight by 30%.

Simply put, body condition scores between 6 and 9 indicate obesity
and carry with them all the risks associated with that condition.
Such dangers include diabetes, high blood pressure and heart
disease, arthritis, bladder and kidney disease, and hepatic lipidosis
or fatty liver disease.

Body condition scores of three or lower could indicate maladies
such as malnourishment, intestinal parasites, or internal organ
malfunctions. A cat with these low body condition scores needs
medical intervention. She is missing crucial foundational body-
building elements, or her body is not using nutritional intake
properly and requires diagnosis to determine the cause.

Some cats go through phases in which they need extra appetite stimulation. After determining general health with their holistic or primary veterinary provider, try some techniques to stimulate your kitty to eat more normally.

Tip #60: Be sure to eliminate obvious reasons for your cat's lack of appetite if they are within your control.

One potential reason your feline friend might have for turning up her nose at the food you offer might be the location of the food. For example, placement too close to the litter box or an area where she feels unsafe could keep her away from the food bowl.

Likewise, if you offer stale or unappealing food or if the bowl is unclean, you should not be surprised if she chooses to regard your offering as inadequate. All these situations are easy enough to remedy.

You can move the food bowl or litter box to a better location, you can throw out old food and replace it with fresher (and safer!) sustenance, and you can keep her bowls sparkling clean, perhaps alternating bowls between feedings to make it easier to keep them uncontaminated and appealing.

Sometimes cats choose not to eat the food their guardians offer because they cannot smell it – due to nasal congestion, a declining sense of smell from aging, or because it simply is not a very smelly formulation. Offering very foul-smelling nourishment to your cat may be unappealing to you, but it is important that your kitty can smell it – for cats, the more it stinks, the more likely they will eat it!

Sometimes warming up the chow a bit can help release the odors – and also helps it become more appealing for a reticent cat because it more closely replicates body temperature, and therefore the experience of eating freshly-caught prey. On the other hand, food served straight from the refrigerator can be unappealing for a finicky feline.

A final suggestion to help stimulate a hesitant cat to eat involves using the cat's internal static energy. Stroking the length of the feline body stimulates energy within them, similar to the static electrical charge that builds upon us when we tread on the carpet.

Slow, firm, but gentle full-body petting can build up energy within his body that your kitty instinctively needs to release. Commonly, cats scratch on their favorite surfaces to discharge this energy, but when faced with a full bowl of food while receiving energy-building strokes, they will sometimes turn to eat the cuisine in front of them to release it.

Grooming

Body and Hair Coat

Tip #61: Pay attention to keeping your cat well-groomed for his optimal well-being.

Grooming is an essential part of feline health, and most cats spend a significant portion of their waking hours grooming their coats and bodies. In fact, grooming is such an essential part of being a cat that a notable indicator of ill health, physical degeneration, or depression is a decline in physical self-care.

Bathing

Because cats spend so much time taking care of their coats and bodies, we usually do not need to help them with bathing, barring the above conditions. In most cases, we should avoid engaging in soap (or shampoo) and water bathing our feline friends, like we usually would with dogs. If necessary, we should only use shampoos formulated for feline pH to avoid causing irritation or other skin conditions.

The notable exceptions to the anti-bathing rule are "hairless" cats like the Sphynx. Because they lack the hair coat of their furry cousins, the oils their bodies produce do not normally distribute without hair to absorb them, and they can become pretty grubby.

For this reason, experts recommend bathing your Sphynx cat every two weeks or so. If their human guardians approach bathing matter-of-factly from the time they are kittens, Sphynx cats usually accept bathing as a routine part of life and generally submit to the ritual with minimal fuss.

Brushing

As we will discuss in more detail in a subsequent chapter concerning mobility challenges, brushing your cat can serve as a great bonding experience between you and your feline buddy. It's not only the elderly and infirm who can appreciate the connection and pleasant physical sensation brushing can create.

Any cat with hair could potentially relish a nice brushing session — and even Sphynx cats might delight in it if you use a brush with very gentle bristles. Some kitties enjoy it, and others would prefer to avoid the brush.

Likewise, different types of brushes and combs elicit various responses from one cat to another. Therefore, you might need to experiment with several different kinds of brushes or combs, depending on your cat's hair type — and preferences.

Some kinds of cats, especially those with long and particularly soft hair, tend to be prone to tangling and matting of the fur. These cats require diligent assistance from their human parents to keep their coats from becoming matted and keep them from ingesting large quantities of their own hair during their regular self-care sessions. If you have a cat with this kind of fur, you should brush her daily to keep her healthy.

Claws

Nail Trimming

Cats in a natural setting generally need not concern themselves with keeping their nails trimmed. After all, they use their claws for all sorts of essential tasks, from hunting their next meal to self-defense to showing the rival down the block who is boss of their territory.

In your home, however, it's a different story. You have all kinds of furnishings on which he can get his claws stuck. It is a source of annoyance for your feline friend and likely for you as well.

To maximize damage control caused by your kitty's nails, keep them nicely trimmed. It will help to preserve your furniture and carpets, as well as your skin! Any parent of a cat who enjoys a good lap kneading session can no doubt attest to the benefits of keeping your kitty's claws well under control.

Scratching

Tip #62: Encourage kitty to scratch on surfaces you both approve.

Your cat will also attempt to do her part to keep her nails in condition as it is natural for her to use them. It's absolutely crucial for her physical and emotional well-being for you to provide outlets for her natural and instinctive need to scratch.

People are often surprised at the various purposes scratching serves for their feline pals. Cats use their claws for stretching and exercise. They also discharge energy buildup and release stress through their claws.

Scratching has additional uses for cats in terms of communication, as their paws contain scent glands. Kitty may not be able to say out loud in human language, "this belongs to me." Still, by scratching and depositing his scent on things he values or on the perimeter of his territory, he is saying exactly that to anyone who would challenge his sense of belonging or ownership of something important to him.

People commonly find that they spend good money on a carpet-covered scratching post, and their cats completely ignore the post they've provided – and instead destroy their favorite sofa or a section of hardwood flooring. Keep in mind that your kitty is an individual with her own tastes and preferences, just like you are.

Some cats favor a horizontal scratching surface, while others like to reach up vertically. Others seem to prefer a variety of available options.

Regardless of surface orientation, one extremely important quality to keep in mind for a scratcher is sturdiness. Cats in outdoor settings commonly scratch on trees or logs that provide a surface that will not tip over and allow them to get great pulling action on the scratch without moving around.

In terms of surfaces, there are plenty of options and types to try. Some kitties do like scratching on carpet-covered posts, but there are also varieties covered in sisal, a rope material that cats enjoy. Alternatively, many cats find cardboard or wood very appealing. It's a good idea to give your feline buddy a good range of options to determine his preferences.

Declawing

Please do not have your cat declawed as a method of saving your furnishings. This surgical procedure was quite popular in years past, but the past is where it belongs.

Research conclusively proves that declawing causes significant physical and social-emotional damage to cats. In fact, the surgery is illegal now in many places, with others increasingly following suit.

The surgery itself is more brutal than many people even realize. It consists of an amputation at what would be the human equivalent of the top knuckle of each finger.

So, it essentially equates to 10 simultaneous amputations because cats have ten toes in the front and eight in the rear. These numbers would naturally increase in the case of polydactyly. It is because a polydactyl cat has the congenital condition of extra toes – and adorable mitten-like paws.

Multiple amputations on the front paws understandably cause great pain to cats manifesting in different ways. For example, even after enduring the initial trauma immediately following the surgery, which in itself is extremely excruciating, comes sensitivity while scratching the substrate in the litter box. As a result, many cats stop using the litter box following declaw surgery because scratching their litter causes them too much pain, and they learn to associate the litter box with discomfort.

Another unintended consequence of losing the front part of their toes is how the absence of digits that should be there changes the cat's gait. Over time, the adjusted movement affects the cat's musculoskeletal system, leading to increased skeletal and arthritic pain. Cats are already prone to mobility challenges in their golden years, but declawing makes it that much worse for them.

Also, consider the safety factor. A cat with no claws loses a crucial means of self-defense, which is why many declawed felines increase their biting behaviors: biting becomes their only defense when they feel threatened.

A declawed cat that accidentally finds himself outdoors is in an exceptionally precarious and vulnerable situation. He cannot use his claws against predators or rivals. Climbing is much more difficult without claws, and he will be slower to escape and therefore at higher risk of predation. In addition, he will have more difficulty hunting to sustain himself without his claws.

As noted above, cats use their claws for multiple reasons. Eliminating their claws robs them of their very feline essence and their ability to express their true, instinctive nature. Although we cannot fault our ancestors for their ignorance, it is selfish and cruel of us to do such a thing to our friends now that we know and understand how destructive it is for them.

Dental Care

Tip #62: Prioritize dental maintenance for an optimal lifetime vitality.

Teeth Brushing

You may be surprised to learn that you can brush your cat's teeth to help keep his dental health in check. You can find dental supplies for cats with an online search or at your local animal supply retailer. Some veterinarians even carry them.

Cat toothbrushes come in a few different types. Some resemble human toothbrushes but with smaller bristle-heads, and they are more ergonomically angled for the feline mouth. Some are dual-headed with a bristle-head at each end. Some even fit over a human finger thimble-style for a more natural-feeling experience.

You should never use human toothpaste with your feline companion as it can be highly toxic. Kitties cannot consume fluoride, so their toothpaste breaks down tartar and bacterial waste using an enzyme formulation that is safe for them to swallow.

Cat toothpaste comes in flavors designed to appeal to the feline taste, such as poultry or malt. It helps to increase your cat's buy-in to the notion of teeth brushing.

Most kitties will resist the process if you suddenly try to brush their teeth one day out of the blue. Ideally, training your little buddy to tolerate a good tooth scrubbing from the time he is very young will help the process go much more smoothly when he is an adult.

Of course, if you acquire him as an adult, you may not have the luxury of such early pliability. If you are starting for the first time with an older kitty, you will need to introduce the idea of tooth brushing in stages to work up to the full routine.

First, you'll need to get him accustomed to having your fingers around and in his mouth; practice rubbing your bare fingers over his teeth and gums. It may take quite a few tries before he adjusts to this feeling.

Next, you can introduce the toothpaste. Allow him to sniff and lick it off your fingers. Next, work up to rub it gently over his teeth and gums with your fingers. Then you can begin to bring in the toothbrush and repeat the previous steps using it until he readily accepts the procedure. It may take quite a while and a lot of patience from you both to get to that point, but your friend's dental health is worth the time and effort.

Dental Treats

If you find that you are unable to get your cat to adjust to the idea of your brushing her teeth, there are treats available on the market that are infused with enzymes similar to those in cat toothpaste. This method of keeping a kitty's teeth clean is less effective than brushing, but some cats will give you no choice.

Veterinary Dental Cleanings

Dental and periodontal diseases are pretty common in cats – and especially in those without the benefit of regular brushing. Leaving tartar buildup and dental disease untreated can cause severe health conditions, so keeping your friend's "smile" bright is of utmost importance.

Once your cat shows signs of tartar buildup and/or dental disease, your veterinarian may suggest a dental cleaning. These cleanings are generally performed under anesthesia, as they are reasonably intensive and require scraping the tartar from beneath the gum line.

As you can imagine, any anesthetic procedure carries with it some risk and a relatively high expense. However, in most cases, you can avoid the need for dental cleanings with diligent home dental care.

Chapter 3 Review

- Providing complete, balanced, and biologically appropriate nutrition is the best way to keep your cat healthy and promote longevity.
- Unlike many other species, felines have very special and unique dietary needs.
- Paying attention to your cat's grooming, such as meticulous skin, hair, and nail maintenance, contributes to a lifetime of vitality.
- Do not underestimate the importance of your cat's claws for physical and social-emotional well-being.

- Diligent dental care for your cat may seem challenging or daunting, or even weird. Still, it is achievable with patience and persistence and is vital for keeping your feline companion healthy.

Chapter 4: Life Cycle Care – Kitten Stage

Just like humans, cats experience their lives differently in the various life stages. Each stage has its own behavioral and health hallmarks. As the being holding the keys to your feline's health and happiness, you alone have the responsibility to set your kitty up for success in each season of his life. In this chapter, we will discuss kittens.

Definition of Kitten

Most people use the general rule of thumb that a feline is full-grown around the one-year mark. It may be a little bit simplistic, as defining the term "kitten" depends on context. Growth and development vary in cats.

For example, cats can reach reproductive maturity when they are between the ages of four and 18 months when considering the possibilities on both extreme ends of the spectrum. As with humans, there is a wide variance in the years they reach pubescence. In terms of behavior and reaching peak physical size, you might consider your young feline a kitten until around 12 to 18 months of age or so.

Advantages and Disadvantages of the Kitten Stage

Advantages

The Adorability Factor

The first and most obvious advantage to bringing a kitten versus an adult cat into your home is the cuteness factor. I may be a little bit biased when I say this, but I think I will garner much agreement: There is no creature on Planet Earth quite as endearing as a kitten. So few people can resist a tiny purring ball of fur and whiskers.

Longevity and Health

Only slightly second in the apparent advantage category is the chronological age of the kitten. You will likely have more time with this small feline than you would with an older cat, and there is something to be said for establishing an early bond to last a lifetime. In conjunction with the notion of age and health, a kitten is less likely to experience a catastrophic illness in the near future than her older counterpart would be.

Tip #63: Begin training early to make life easier for you and your kitty throughout your cat's lifetime.

Tolerance for Learning and Adaptability

Perhaps a bit less obvious is your ability to train a young cat in the rules and quirks of your household unencumbered by the baggage of a former full life with another person or family. Additionally, this is the ideal time to train your little feline to easily accept the essential handling he will experience with health care and any other imperatives you would like to instill in his youth.

For example, life will be infinitely easier for you and your cat throughout his life if he has positive associations with the carrier. A kitten, having limited experience with carriers, likely has not yet developed the negative associations so many older cats might have and will therefore be easier to train.

Similarly, training your young feline to come when called can make any number of scenarios much more manageable and could even be a lifesaver in the case of future emergencies. From the convenience of having your cat respond immediately to your having called him for dinner to the downright urgency of needing to gather him for an emergency evacuation, you will thank yourself for training him in his youth to come when you call him.

You and your cat's health care team will benefit from your prescience in teaching the kitty to tolerate having his body parts handled individually. For example, suppose he learns early to accept having his paws manipulated calmly. In that case, your future attempts to trim his nails will be simple and successful, and you can avoid the bloodshed many cat guardians encounter when trying to trim claws on a less-than-willing feline. Less bloodshed is good!

The same story holds true with other common procedures. For example, suppose the veterinarian can touch a kitty all over his body, including looking into his mouth. In that case, they will be able to conduct more thorough examinations and will undoubtedly appreciate your foresight and willingness to train your cat from an early age.

Young kittens will generally accept other animals and unknown people more readily than will an older cat and likely will require less adjustment and introduction time if you plan to integrate her with another cat, kitten, animal companion, or person.

Disadvantages

Please note that while exceptionally adorable, a kitten does come with some disadvantages in contrast with an adult cat. For one thing, kittens require quite a bit of attention, as a young human child does.

Tip #64: Kitten-proof your home for safety and to secure your possessions.

Kitten-Proofing

Young felines explore their environments with their mouths and physically explore every corner, nook, and cranny they can find. So you must kitten-proof, similarly to how you would toddler-proof for safety, and pay close attention to their whereabouts at all times.

When going through the kitten-proofing process, remember to try to envision the environment from the perspective of a tiny, curious being. A kitten will occupy all the various levels of your home, getting into places you might not even think to secure because you see the house from the perspective and eye level of an adult human.

Now that you have a feline in your house, it's a good idea anyway to adjust to the new normal of viewing the world from your cat's perspective. It will help you understand the cat in your life from this point forward and can only serve to enhance the relationship between the two of you.

High Energy Levels

Tip #65: Two kittens can be easier than one.

Kittens have seemingly boundless energy, and until they grow up a bit and understand the routine in your household, they may keep you up at night with their boisterous antics. Additionally, their high energy levels can lead to the destruction of your favorite things as they seek to entertain themselves.

If you think you might like to adopt two cats, consider adopting two kittens together so that they can expend their boundless energies upon one another. In addition, they will keep each other entertained. In general, two kittens can be far easier than one!

More Frequent Veterinary Visits

Kittens require more routine veterinary care to ensure a healthy start than most adult cats might, as adults are likely already on an annual exam and vaccine schedule. In addition, vaccines require boosters in immature cats, so diligent cat parents will bring them to the vet several times for routine care within their first year.

Adults are also generally less physically vulnerable than their young counterparts, having passed the critical developmental stages and grown to their full size and weight. However, with their tiny stature and adventurous behaviors, kittens can more easily fall victim to accidental injury than a full-grown cat.

Hallmarks and Details of the Kitten Stage

Becoming a Cat

The primary job of a kitten is learning "how to cat," according to colloquial reference, and within the context of sharing your life, he simultaneously learns what it means to live in your household. Because we control the environment, it's essential that we set up the surroundings that will help our young feline blossom into a fully actualized cat.

In terms of DNA, cats are not very far removed from their wild ancestors, so for them to be happy and live their authentic lives, they need to be able to express their ancestral feline tendencies. Those instincts are deeply ingrained and for humans to fight against them is not only fruitless but cruel and arrogant. Therefore, your kitten will express herself in increasingly catlike ways as she matures.

Tip #66: Try to see your cat's or kitten's living environment from a feline perspective to set her up for successful integration.

Look at each room in your kitten's environment through a feline lens and provide proper outlets for natural behaviors. For example, kittens are very active and climb everything in sight, likely including things you would rather they didn't climb – like your designer curtains or your leg!

It is okay to set limits and remove your kitten from places you would prefer he didn't climb, but it is also critical to replace the behavior you want to curb with a behavior that you find acceptable. For example, in the case of a kitten climbing your pants leg, when you remove the kitten from your leg, you will need a good alternative place for him to climb – and providing a reward for climbing there is the key to reinforcing that behavior. The more acceptable options you provide for your kitten, the better his chances for success and the less aggravation for you.

Tip #67: Provide many appropriate outlets for play behavior.

You may have noticed that kittens will turn every little object into a toy. Sometimes they even seem to be playing with invisible or imaginary toys. Play behavior in kittens is an instinctive precursor to learning how to hunt and is critical for their growth and development, as well as for fostering their very feline essence, even if they will never have to hunt to eat.

To the developing feline, play equals prey. So be sure to provide a wide variety of play outlets for independent and interactive play to replicate the wild hunting instinct, nurturing the ancestral cat within.

One principal caveat: Although some people find it cute and tempting to play with their kittens using their hands or feet, such behavior teaches the kitten habits that will be difficult to break and will become problematic as the kitten reaches maturity. Be sure that all toys are inanimate objects and not human body parts.

Ideally, your kitten will have learned the basics of feline behavior from her mother and siblings. These lessons include learning limits in play interactions, such as acceptable levels of biting and scratching. You need to set similar limits and redirect behavior that you find unacceptable to more suitable outlets, like toys she enjoys.

Tip #68: Puzzle feeders provide additional expression of crucial feline behaviors.

Another appropriate outlet you can provide to help develop and pacify the hunting instinct is a set of puzzle feeders so that your kitten can engage his brain in order to access some of his food or treats. It closely replicates the behavior of your kitty's wild ancestors: hunting and foraging for food.

Every day the natural survival behavior of a wild cat includes repeating a ritual several times every day. This ritual is universal within feline species and includes – in order: hunt or stalk, catch, kill, eat, groom, and sleep – repeat.

Solving a puzzle to get to a meal or treat engages his brain similarly through the first four stages of the ritual and helps provide necessary enrichment for your young cat. Because kittens learn rapidly, it is best to have several kinds of puzzles and rotate them frequently to ensure the novelty to keep the kitty engaged and interested.

Special Nutritional Needs

Tip #69: Feed your kitten a diet specially formulated for the needs of her growing and developing body.

Speaking of mealtimes, another hallmark of the kitten stage of life is special nutritional needs for your kitty to grow into a healthy adult cat. After all, she is rapidly increasing in size, and she expends a tremendous amount of energy in learning about her body and her world.

Caloric needs are higher for kittens than for adult cats, and they generally need to eat several meals daily to keep up with their comparatively higher nutritional needs. In addition to greater caloric intake is the need for more protein as their muscle mass increases. In fact, about 30% of a kitten's caloric intake should come from protein. A higher ratio of amino acids and some vitamins and minerals also supports a kitten's growing body.

For these reasons, you should feed your little feline friend a diet formulated especially for kittens. Studies indicate that, like human children, kittens offered a variety of flavor profiles, textures, and kinds of foods will more readily accept unfamiliar foods throughout their lifetimes. Therefore, provide a variety of healthful foods to your little kitty to avoid raising a picky eater, which could be problematic once he is an adult or senior cat. You may transition him in slow increments to a nutritious adult cat food beginning in the 12-month to 18-month age range.

Health Care Needs

As previously noted, kittens require more frequent veterinary visits for preventative health care. For kittens, such visits are primarily for routine exams as their bodies grow and change, vaccine boosters, and parasite detection and treatment.

Regardless of the persistent myth that having received colostrum in mother's milk gives sufficient immunity against diseases, a kitten should begin her vaccine series by around six to eight weeks of age. They do receive antibodies from their mother's milk, but the antibody effects wane over time, necessitating vaccinations.

Tip #70: Be sure to complete your kitten's initial vaccine series and keep vaccinations current – especially in the case of potential exposure to other cats or kittens. She is vulnerable until she has completed the series and should avoid any possible exposure risk beforehand.

We'll describe each one of the necessary feline vaccines below. The most common vaccinations for kittens include the FVRCP vaccine, the FeLV vaccine, and the rabies vaccine. If you would like additional information about feline vaccine guidelines and would like to do research independent of your veterinarian, you can check out the website for the American Animal Hospital Association (AAHA.org) under feline vaccination guidelines. We'll provide the web address in the reference section.

FVRCP

First, let's discuss FVRCP. This vaccine protects your kitten against three diseases in one joint injection. FVR stands for Feline Viral Rhinotracheitis, or, alternatively, Feline herpesvirus type-1. The kind of herpes virus that infects cats is not transmissible to humans but is highly contagious to other cats.

Cats of all ages are susceptible to this virus, which presents similarly to a cold or pneumonia. Its effects can range from mild cold-type symptoms to fatal in young kittens. Like the herpes virus that affects humans, it can live dormant within your kitten or cat and never truly goes away.

Once the virus lives inside its host, the only course of action is to minimize the severity of the symptoms and the frequency with which they occur. It is possible to manage the symptoms, and most cats can live long and healthy lives with the virus, but of course, this is not ideal, and the vaccine can help prevent your kitty from becoming infected.

Another viral infection that affects the upper respiratory tract in cats and kittens is Calicivirus – the "C" in FVRCP. Like Feline Viral Rhinotracheitis, Calicivirus is a herpes virus: Felid alphaherpesvirus 1. The same information applies to both diseases.

Feline Panleukopenia, the "P" in FVRCP, is a different type of virus. It doesn't affect the upper respiratory system but instead usually presents mainly with symptoms in the intestinal tract, such as severe vomiting and bloody diarrhea. The actual pathology of the disease is a severe decline in white blood cells, the immunity cells that protect your kitty from infections and diseases.

Panleukopenia is the feline version of the parvovirus and generally affects kittens more readily than it does adult cats. It is a highly contagious disease and is environmentally hardy, meaning it can live in the environment for a long time if not properly destroyed.

Panleukopenia is difficult for a kitten to survive, and you should take it very seriously if your kitten displays the symptoms: listlessness, vomiting, diarrhea, dull-looking coat, and dehydration. Although it is a viral infection and therefore cannot be eliminated directly, your kitten can survive it if you catch it early enough and provide the veterinary-aided support her little body needs, including aggressive fluid treatment and antibiotics to prevent secondary bacterial infections.

Again though, the best thing is to prevent the disease in the first place by completing the FVRCP vaccine series. For kittens, the initial FVRCP vaccine happens ideally at around age six to eight weeks and requires three boosters, one booster each month until the series is complete.

Your kitten is not fully protected until after her final booster is complete. When your kitty reaches adulthood, she will only need this vaccine once every year or every three years, depending on the schedule you and your veterinarian determine together based on lifestyle factors.

FeLV

The FeLV vaccine protects your kitten from Feline Leukemia. You may be familiar with the human version of leukemia, which is a type of cancer. In cats, it is a virus that primarily diminishes the immune system but can develop into cancer in the future. Therefore, it may not kill a cat or kitten outright, but it can lead to your feline friend contracting another disease that can prove fatal.

Feline Leukemia cannot be passed from cats to humans but is contagious from one cat to another through the transmission of fluids like nasal fluids or saliva. Cats in close, regular contact sharing food or water bowls or litter boxes can catch it from one another, but it is most readily passed through fighting.

Similar to a herpes virus, the feline leukemia virus lives within the body throughout the cat's lifetime. Therefore, a FeLV-positive diagnosis does not necessarily mean your kitty cannot live a full and productive life. Still, it does mean that you will need to be diligent to prevent spreading it to other cats, and to protect your cat or kitten from potential secondary disease and infection. You will also need to watch your kitty closely for any signs of illness and address them immediately with a veterinarian.

To prevent your kitten from contracting Feline Leukemia, you may begin her vaccine series at six to 12 weeks of age and give a booster three to four weeks later. This vaccine is only a series of two injections. Once your kitty reaches adulthood, you and your veterinarian may determine together that she only needs the FeLV vaccine annually, every three years, or perhaps not at all, depending on lifestyle factors. Be sure to discuss the schedule with your cat's health care team.

Rabies

Unlike the other common feline vaccines, the vaccine for the rabies virus is a public health requirement because rabies is a zoonotic disease, meaning it is transmissible from non-human animals to humans. It is why your veterinarian will issue a rabies vaccination certificate when giving the vaccine to your cat, so you can prove that your cat has been inoculated to protect him and anyone he may inadvertently bite from contracting the rabies virus.

Fortunately, the rabies vaccine does not need a booster for a full year. After that, in most municipalities, you can move to a schedule of rabies vaccines every three years for your kitty as long as you keep up-to-date on her rabies vaccine schedule. However, requirements vary from one place to another, so check with your veterinarian and follow their recommendations.

Chapter 4 Review:

- You can consider your young feline a kitten until the age of 12 to 18 months, but she could reach sexual maturity and experience her first estrus to be capable of reproduction at as young as four months of age.
- Some advantages of adopting a kitten versus an adult cat include some obvious benefits, including how cute they are, their health, and the number of years you will likely have together. Additional rewards can consist of early training without baggage from a former life and potentially easier integration with other animals or people.
- Kittens also come with some disadvantages, including needing extra attention and kitten-proofing your home to ensure safety and minimize household destruction. Your little ball of fluff will have a great deal of energy and may even keep you awake at night.
- The primary job of a kitten is to learn how to grow into a healthy and successful cat. To ensure a positive, well-adjusted maturing experience, provide an environment well-suited to foster the wild animal within your kitten as he grows.
- Kittens have higher nutritional and health care requirements in contrast to adult cats. So be sure to feed them appropriately and take them for their recommended exams and vaccine visits to ensure a healthy foundation to build their lives and bodies.

Chapter 5: Life Cycle Care – Prime Adult Stage

Definition of Prime Adult Cat

Once your kitty has reached approximately 12 to 18 months of age, leaving behind his kitten stage, he becomes a young adult. It is when his routines and the extra care and attention he once needed will level out into a predictable rhythm. He will remain in the "Prime Adult Cat" category – indicating a full-grown cat in his prime of life – until he reaches approximately ten years old.

Advantages and Disadvantages of the Prime Adult Stage

Advantages

By now, your little house feline knows the ropes and no longer needs to discover through taking everything into his mouth. So you can relax a little bit with the extra attention a wee one needs.

If you have adopted a cat in this stage of life, you were likely able to skip the kitty-proofing altogether, with a reduced need for vigilance. Of course, be sure to assess the environment for safety since cats are notoriously curious, but they are significantly less trouble-seeking than their younger counterparts. In addition, it is the most relaxed stage for cat-guardianship as a whole, as adults in the prime of life have no special age-related needs.

Disadvantages

This stage, to be frank, really has no significant disadvantages. Perhaps you miss the sweet, clumsy, energetic kitten that once shared your home, but she is now a sleek, beautiful version of her former self with more knowledge of the ways of the world, and she still has plenty of playful energy.

Nutrition: Adult Cat Food

Tip #71: Transition a young adult cat from kitten food to adult cat food to avoid caloric intake that exceeds his energetic requirements.

At this point, if you have not yet transitioned your young feline to an adult formula cat food, it is time to do so, as he is no longer in the process of growing his body into its adult state. As a result, he no longer needs the higher calories, extra protein, or additional vitamins and minerals that he needed while he was growing so rapidly. Continuing to feed him the diet that helped him grow to his adult size will surpass his caloric needs and could lead to obesity, which is an unhealthy state for anybody – human or non-human.

You may find that he wants fewer snacks throughout the day than he did when he was a little kitty, although the feline body is designed to ingest frequent small meals all day long, so there is no need to discourage him from frequent snacking. Just ensure the snacks are healthy and suitable for an adult cat. Continue to use food puzzles to help him minimize his consumption and mimic the natural feline hunting behavior for his behavioral enrichment.

Tip #72: Change your cat's diet slowly to avoid tummy troubles.

Even though you may have been feeding your cat a variety of foods, the kitty might experience intestinal upset associated with abrupt dietary change any time you introduce something new. To transition your cat from one kind of food to another, including a simple brand switch sometime down the road, you should make the change or introduce the new food gradually.

For a smooth transition, mix a combination of the new food into the old food. Start with a small quantity of the novel diet. Then, each day, slightly increase the amount of the new food while decreasing the old food. Converting from one diet to another might take approximately one week from beginning to end.

Exercise and Feline Fulfillment

As your kitten transforms into a full-grown cat, you may notice that she seems a little bit less playful than she was previously. It is entirely normal. Remember, kittens play to learn, exercise, and express the hunting behavior deeply ingrained in them from their wild ancestry. She no longer needs to learn how to become an adult cat, removing the educational component of her need for play. She has arrived into her full feline nature!

Tip #73: Do not underestimate the power and essential nature of playtime and your role in it.

Your cat still needs to play to satisfy the remaining two components to its necessity, possibly even more so. In addition, her need for exercise may have increased as her metabolism has likely slowed somewhat.

As her caretaker, you are responsible for helping her get enough exercise to burn off the calories that she is not burning off as naturally as she did when she was tiny. It means that it may take a little more work and effort from you to stimulate the prey drive in her and help her get enough activity now that she is an adult.

Just as her need for encouragement to exercise increases as she enters adulthood, so does her need for feline expression. She is now a fully actualized cat and needs to express her feline nature to feel inherently fulfilled. You can help by ensuring she has everything she needs within her environment to express herself as a cat.

Tip #74: Environmental enrichment and perceived safety are vital to your cat's mental and emotional health, and as her caretaker and provider who controls her environment, you are responsible for supplying them.

She needs appropriate items that she enjoys scratching. She needs places both for climbing and for "caving" – or getting away from the hustle and bustle of life. She needs to feel comfortable and safe in her environment. She needs various kinds of stimulation to keep her mind alert and her body active between naps.

Cat TV

Tip #75: *Give your kitty stimulating, species-appropriate activities to fill her days.*

To stimulate her mind, you can provide "Cat TV" in both natural and simulated forms. For example, a natural form of Cat TV might involve a bird and/or squirrel feeder outside a window where she can sit comfortably and watch the natural activity outside. Even if it is not feasible to place a feeder directly outside a window, she will likely appreciate having access to sit or lie comfortably by a window where she can watch the activity outside.

An example of simulated Cat TV might literally involve television. If you have a tv or tablet that can stream videos from the internet, you can play videos to intrigue your kitty. Of course, some cats enjoy screen time, and some respond less enthusiastically, but it is worth checking out as a form of enrichment.

Tip #76: *If you use a television or a tablet to engage your cat, be sure to keep the sound on to invigorate your cat's senses further and generate more interest. Cats are sensory-driven.*

Videos of birds and squirrels, mice, other rodents, and even fish are available and free to stream. She may even enjoy watching videos of other cats engaging in feline activities. So experiment a little bit to determine your cat's favorite subjects to watch.

Some videos you can find online will play for up to 12 hours, so if you are gone during the day, you might consider playing them as an option to engage your cat, perhaps switching up the programming daily to keep things novel and exciting for your kitty.

Personal Interaction

Tip #77: Having a large variety of toys and activities around for your cat to engage with is great but cannot fully replace time spent playing with you.

To stimulate your cat's body and promote bonding with her, you should make a daily habit of playing with her using interactive types of toys or games that she enjoys. Experiment with different kinds of toys and games to find out what really gets her feline predator juices going.

Wand toys are an excellent choice, as you can use the toy to mimic the movements of common feline prey animals like rodents, birds, or insects without putting your body parts in danger of an errant claw or bite. Imitating the actions of wounded prey or prey that hides can be especially exciting for a cat.

As noted previously, cats respond to stimuli that engage their senses. Adding sounds that feline prey might make – like the rustling of tissue paper, for example, can intensify the appeal. A toy moving at the end of a wand string is a lot of fun, but it becomes even more alluring when it behaves, sounds, or looks like something that the cat would want to chase and eat in the wild.

Tip #78: With their enhanced sense of hearing, cats respond well to hushed noises – similar to the sounds a prey animal might produce.

Surprisingly, some cats can even enjoy a good game of fetch with their favorite humans, chasing after small light items that they can easily retrieve using their mouths. Use a variety of toys to keep the games novel and retain your cat's interest. Pay attention to the toys to which your kitty naturally gravitates.

So how much should you play with your cat? The general rule of thumb is about 20 minutes of interactive play daily. Some cats might need more extended sessions, and some might want several shorter sessions over the course of the day. Let your cat dictate how much she wants you to play with her, and remember that even

86

when she is not physically running, jumping, or pouncing, the play has value.

Tip #79: Be willing to defer to your cat's style of play, even if you find it less exciting than your own.

Watching, hiding from, and stalking the prey are also valuable feline play behaviors. It helps satisfy your cat's exercise and mental-emotional health requirements if each play session consists of several bouts of high energy play followed by play that is lower key, alternating between the two until your cat decides she is finished.

It may get boring watching your cat stalking the toy you are dragging across the floor instead of pouncing on it, but she is still benefiting from that behavior, as it is similar to what she would do while hunting. Remember, the play session is for your cat's benefit, not for your entertainment.

Tip #80: Read your cat's body language to determine interest level and engagement.

Sometimes it is difficult for humans to read feline expressions and body language. So you may wonder if your cat is even interested in the toy you are holding when she is not actively engaged in grabbing at it, chasing after it, or pouncing on it. Some indicators that she is engaged include: intense staring at and tracking of an object, whiskers pointing forward toward the object (rather than out to the sides as they would be in a normal, relaxed state), ears that face ahead toward the object, and body crouching low in "pounce" position. These are all signs of feline interest.

Tip #81: Cats are creatures of habit and respond well to routines.

If you have the ability to do so, make playtime part of a routine. You will find that your kitty's internal clock is very accurate, as cats thrive on routine. As a result, she will likely seek you out to remind you of important events in her day, such as playtime and mealtime!

Adult Cat Veterinary Care

As mentioned in the previous chapter, one of the benefits of living with an adult cat versus a kitten is that you can scale back his visits to the veterinarian now that he has fully grown. Barring any complications or concerns that may arise, adult cats in their prime generally only need their general wellness exams once a year.

Tip #82: Continue visits to veterinary professionals at least annually.

Depending on the schedule you and your cat's health team determine together based on his lifestyle and disease exposure risks, the kitty may only need vaccines once every several years. However, it is still a good idea to bring him in for a wellness exam annually, including a stool sample to check for parasites.

Cats tend to be instinctually stoic animals and naturally hide signs of illness. It is a holdover from their wild roots. In the wild, any sign of weakness can spell catastrophe for them if a predator or rival can detect it, so cats evolved a great talent and propensity for masking their illnesses and injuries for the purposes of self-preservation. Health practitioners know how to recognize concerns that your cat may be instinctively hiding.

Tip #83: Keep in mind your cat's comparatively accelerated aging process to maintain an accurate perspective regarding the need for wellness examinations.

Compared to humans, cats have significantly shorter life spans. It translates to a comparatively accelerated aging process. You may have heard that every year equals seven years for a dog or a cat, but this is an overly simplified and misleading rule of thumb. The American Association of Feline Practitioners (AAFP) and the American Animal Hospital Association (AAHA) agree on an estimate of cat years to human years.

Kittens having graduated to adult cat status at one year of age are equivalent to a human at 15 years old. In the following year, your cat ages approximately another nine years, bringing him to a maturity level roughly comparable to a 24-year-old human. Each year thereafter corresponds roughly to about four human years.

Thinking about this accelerated aging process, it should be no surprise that your cat should have a wellness evaluation at least annually as an adult in his prime. Finding issues and concerns early is the best way to maintain your cat's health over his lifetime.

Chapter 5 Review:

- Cats are adults in the prime portion of their lives from the approximate ages of one year to 10 years old.
- Convert to adult food and continue using slow and puzzle feeders to minimize the risk of developing obesity. Transition your kitty slowly to new foods to avoid the intestinal upset that can occur with abrupt dietary change.
- Once your cat reaches adulthood, play is still important. Exercise needs to increase when metabolism decreases to help prevent obesity. Play also helps to satisfy the core hunting instincts cats retain from their wild ancestry and supports the bond with their guardians.
- You should provide appropriate enrichment for your cat to promote an alert mind and active body. Use a variety of kinds of stimulation to do so. For example, you can provide interesting things for your cat to watch. Predictable and reliable playtime with you is also essential.
- You can scale back veterinary wellness exams to once a year when your cat reaches the adult stage. However, those annual exams are still important, even when lifestyle indicates kitty does not need vaccines every year. It is because cats age more rapidly than humans do. They also hide the signs of illness or injury, so we might miss important indicators of infirmity that a veterinary professional might detect.

Chapter 6: Life Cycle Care – Senior and Super-Senior Stage

Definitions of Senior and Super-Senior or Geriatric

When your cat has been alive on our planet for about 10 to 11 years, he begins entering the senior portion of his life. His routines and care have been relatively steady and stable for a good chunk of time, barring unusual health challenges. Still, now that he's progressing in age, he may be slowing down a bit, and some of his organs and bodily systems may begin to need support to keep functioning properly.

As he nears geriatric or super-senior age, generally around 15 years old, the deceleration of his body and movements may become more apparent. He is no longer the fully vital cat in the prime of life that he was before, but he may still have quite a bit more life to live. He certainly still has plenty of love to offer.

Advantages and Disadvantages of the Senior Stages

Advantages

If your senior cat has been living with you in your household for a long time, she knows and understands the rules and routines. Life and behaviors are relatively stable and predictable by this point. Her high-energy days are behind her, and she is content to nap in a sunbeam. She's already "cooked."

Adopting a cat in the waning portion of her life can yield a surprisingly rewarding experience. She'll likely bestow loads of love and gratitude on you for taking her in and giving her your love and comfort in her sunset years. Whereas kittens might take such a blessing for granted, seniors, in particular, understand the significance of being adopted into a loving home, and they do respond in kind with gratitude.

Disadvantages

Tip #84: Pay close attention to your cat's health and changing needs, increasing veterinary visits in the elder stage of life.

Sadly, like humans and all other animals, cats have increased health challenges as they age - their need for veterinary care increases. You may need to treat known age-related conditions. Even if you are unaware of specific health concerns, the need for regular wellness exams increases to help you diagnose issues you might otherwise overlook. When the kitty reaches an advanced age, he should visit his health care team at least twice annually for those well cat exams.

You may need to make some alterations to his home environment to accommodate his deteriorating body and keep his quality of life intact. Sometimes facing the prospect of declining wellness and future loss of our sweet feline companions can additionally cause us distress and turmoil. We owe it to our cats to put in the effort on their behalf.

Hallmarks and Details of Senior Life Stages

As with most animals, the earliest stages of feline life signify growth and development of the body, mind, senses, and social tolerance. Likewise, the latest phases represent the decline and degeneration of the same – in human and non-human animals alike, including cats.

Bodily, Sensory, and Mental Decline

Besides the extremely early stages of kitten-hood, the final 10 percent tends to represent the most fragile time in your cat's life. It is not to say that you should simply chalk up physical ailments to normal aging and discount them as irreversible or untreatable.

Nothing could be further from the truth. We owe it to our cats to keep them healthy and comfortable as long as we can, and many conditions can be alleviated or even reversed.

Every cat, regardless of age, should have regular veterinary visits. As previously stated, you should bring him to visit his health care team twice annually for wellness checks to preserve or improve the quality of life for your feline friend in his sunset years. But also be sure to address discernable behavioral or health changes as soon as you notice them.

Remember the talent and tendency cats have for hiding their illness and pain and their rapid aging process, which can advance maladies quickly. Once you become aware of something amiss, he is likely to have been suffering from the ailment for a while. Time is of the essence for our elder feline companions.

Tip #85: Don't let your senior cat be the victim of the common practice of waiting for illness to visit the veterinarian.

In a study across approximately 1500 veterinary hospitals and 1.5 million animals, researchers discovered that of the animals brought in to the vet across the research period due to illness, 48% of the cats had not seen the veterinarian for the preceding 18 months, and 42% had not been examined by veterinary staff for three years.

In that period, conditions that might have been treatable if caught early could become irreversible. At the very least, guardians could avoid months' worth of pain and discomfort for their cats with more frequent health care visits. It is patently unfair for us to put our cats through potentially avoidable pain for our own convenience, cost-saving, or unwillingness to face unpleasantness.

Such visits allow veterinary professionals to assess your cat's range of motion, weight, muscle tone, and bodily systems to track degenerative changes as they occur. Commonly, a veterinarian will evaluate your kitty's bloodwork, urine, and stool to look for changes or concerns, as those are the most reliable diagnostic tools at the disposal of health care teams.

Degeneration is often difficult or impossible to detect without these tools that are available only to veterinary practitioners. You see your kitty every day, and even though you love him, you are unlikely to notice changes that occurred slowly over the long term.

Additional items of concern for a thorough health evaluation, perhaps receiving more emphasis from a holistic or integrative veterinarian, will include assessing nutrition, supplements and activity levels, and possibly suggestions for ongoing therapeutic treatments. All of these factors can increase your kitty's quality of remaining life if assessed and prescribed by a skilled integrative or holistic practitioner.

Tip #85: Look for behavioral changes which can signal that your cat might benefit from veterinary attention, whether from a holistic veterinarian, a traditional veterinarian, or an integrated combination approach.

Degenerative Conditions Common in Felines

Decreased Mobility

You might notice some subtle behavioral signals that could indicate the more urgent need for a visit with your kitty's health care team than the biannual scheduled maintenance. For example, if she seems hesitant to jump onto areas she once frequented, or if she makes attempts to jump and fails to execute the leap successfully, your cat might be experiencing joint pain, muscle deterioration, or generalized difficulty with mobility.

Similarly, if she begins eliminating outside the litter box, it could also point to degenerative muscle and joint disease like arthritis, if she has discomfort or difficulty getting into the box or it is located inconveniently for her. Arthritis is unusually common in older cats.

Tip #86: Be accommodating of your senior cat's decreased mobility by adapting her environment to meet her changing needs.

In fact, over 90% of senior cats deal with decreased mobility at some level. Therefore, it amplifies the importance of providing low-sided litter boxes. If you suspect your elder cat may have developed some mobility issues, be mindful and accommodating to ease her access to all of her significant resources.

Place multiple low-sided litter boxes strategically in easily accessible locations on each floor of the home you share with her. Make sure all the litter boxes are easy for her to access.

She may still feel more secure in elevated areas but have difficulty jumping up to them. Provide her with ramps and stairs to help her access areas that are significant to her.

Be sure that she can easily access her food and water bowls. If you have previously provided her food and water in an elevated location – for example, if she needs to jump up to a high place to eat so that the family dog does not steal her food – consider changing the environment by providing her with a ramp or stairs to that site.

Tip #86: Consider installing a cat-friendly baby gate if the home environment has a dog or small child.

Alternatively, you could cordon off a room specifically for your cat if she is significantly smaller than the dog. You can find gates tailored to this very need – with smaller gates built into them so that your cat can go through, but Fido cannot. If you own your home and are handy with tools, you could even install a small cat door or wall pass-through for a more permanent solution than a gate.

As an added bonus, an elder kitty can use this room to escape young children who cannot operate the gates. An older cat has a lower tolerance for the exuberance and enthusiasm of very small children and is more fragile than her younger, more vital counterparts and more vulnerable to being physically harmed. Therefore, a separate escape room is essential for elder felines in such situations.

Tip #87: Purchase an elevated bowl set for your elder friend's physical comfort while eating and drinking.

Returning to the topic of food and water, elevated bowl systems are available for purchase so that your feline friend can eat in a position more parallel to her natural stance, rather than craning her neck down to munch. In addition, such systems help to minimize neck stiffness and vomiting. These setups are beneficial to a cat at all stages of life, especially in your kitty's twilight years when leaning down to eat a meal is likely to cause her pain or aggravate underlying digestive challenges.

Tip #88: Assist your kitty with the coat grooming tasks he once handled easily for himself.

Besides a stiff gait and difficulty jumping to areas that once presented no problems, you may notice your cat's coat seems less sleek and clean than it once was. As cats age and begin to encounter discomfort or difficulty with grooming, they will sometimes groom themselves less heartily, enthusiastically, and frequently than they did in their spry youth.

It is prevalent for overweight cats that may have trouble reaching some areas of their expanded bodies that they could once get. Aging then exacerbates the problem as flexibility of muscles and joints declines and the discomfort associated with grooming increases.

You can and should assist your cat with grooming if he is amenable to the help. Brushing can be a great bonding experience and helps dislodge and dispose of loose hair that might otherwise wind up in your cat's intestinal tract.

Bonded cats often engage in allogrooming – the term used to describe social grooming that occurs between animals of the same species. It serves to simultaneously reinforce their social bonds and their physical and emotional well-being. In cats, it presents as licking each other, primarily around the head and face, but in other areas as well.

Your elder cat might appreciate the grooming from you and interpret it as an allogrooming gesture. But, of course, I recommend using a brush and/or comb to complete this task, rather than your tongue!

Supplementation and Physical Therapy for Arthritis

A plethora of medications, supplements, and physical treatments exist to assist with your kitty's age-related mobility decline and pain. A holistic practitioner can recommend the best combination of supplements and therapies for your kitty's individual needs.

Supplements run the gamut from glucosamine, antioxidants, and omega-3 fats to natural anti-inflammatories that are safe for the feline system. Be sure to always get the recommendation of a feline health professional before giving any medication or supplement to your cat.

Your cat's holistic practitioner might suggest supplements to support your feline friend through the decline of her internal organs and/or cognitive functioning. One supplement that can perform both functions is SAM-e (S-adenosylmethionine), which is proven to decrease mental decline and simultaneously help with liver detoxification while also increasing mobility.

Other supplements that help detoxify organs include plant-based offerings such as dandelion, milk thistle, chlorophyll, and spirulina. In addition, medium-chain triglycerides like coconut oil (which can also assist with passing hairballs) support healthy brain function. Be sure to consult your holistic or integrative veterinary health team to get their recommendations and the best dosages for your feline family member.

Physical therapy might include massage to help relieve stiffness in the joints and increase circulation. The added bonus of massage is that it can help maintain muscle tone, which tends to decline with age, and it can also assist with lymphatic drainage.

Some holistic practitioners may alternatively or additionally recommend practices such as acupuncture, red light therapy, and/or reiki treatments to help with mobility and body pain. To research these procedures, refer to the resources section for links to more information about them.

Elimination Changes

Changes in elimination behaviors are relatively common with advancing age and might manifest either physical or mental challenges. But, unfortunately, there is no one single reason that a cat might eliminate on the floor – or your pillow, or any number of places – instead of inside his litterbox.

There could be a wide range of reasons indicating physical illness for the behavioral variation. For example, urinary tract issues and kidney disease seem to plague cats more readily than other animals in their senior years and can cause changes in elimination behavior. Arthritis that makes litter box use uncomfortable can do the same.

Additionally, as with humans, mental conditions can decline with age in cats as well. Dementia can set in and contribute to changes in elimination habits as your kitty drifts in and out of confusion. Alternatively, such changes could simply result from your cat's reaction to changes within the household that may need to be addressed, as aging also tends to reduce tolerance to upset.

Night Howling

A curious but relatively common symptom of various age-related and degenerative disorders is the onset of night howling or night calling. It can be jarring and irritating to be awakened to the sound of your precious feline friend walking around your home calling or howling in the wee hours of the night for what seems to you like no good reason.

You should be aware that this new behavior can indicate a variety of potential health issues, including urinary tract infection or hypertension. However, such root causes are not necessarily permanent and can be treatable with a proper diagnosis.

A decline in cognitive function or age-related sensory confusion could also be at the root of the behavior, especially at night when the home is dark, and things may suddenly seem unfamiliar to your cat, whose senses, including her vision, have been on the decline. She could simply be confused about where she is or where you are.

Bad Breath

Sudden onset of bad breath could be an indication of dental decline that needs to be addressed. Cats often become victims of periodontal disease, which in itself can be painful, as gums inflame and make eating uncomfortable. Oral abscesses can form due to untreated periodontal disease and can also cause painful bone infections.

Dental disease can surprisingly lead to a variety of other health problems, seemingly unrelated to the mouth. For example, untreated dental disease can surprisingly lead to infection in other organs if bacteria from the mouth enter the bloodstream through diseased mouth tissue. The heart and kidneys are organs commonly affected by untreated, periodontal disease in this manner.

Hiding

When cats feel vulnerable for any reason, they are prone to hiding. As previously discussed, it is in the feline nature to hide their pain, injury, or illness as an instinctive protective measure from predators and rivals.

If an illness is too advanced or painful for your kitty to mask, she may alternatively choose to hide. Hiding that is not normally in your feline friend's behavioral repertoire is a strong indicator that something is very wrong, and she needs to visit her health care team to determine the reason she is suddenly squirreling herself away from the world.

Stress and Emotional Health

Tip #89: Stress is particularly damaging to your cat's physical, mental, and emotional health and is especially essential to minimize.

Stress is bad for everyone, but few species, if any, bear more of its brunt than do cats, who are hard-wired as both prey and predator, regardless of how safe their home situation or how much food is available to them. Each designation comes with its own unique set of stressors.

Cats as Prey

You may notice that your cat always seems to be on high alert. Even when you think she is sleeping, you may see the pinnae or outer portion of her ears swiveling in the direction of sounds in the environment, instinctively aware of any changes that could signal the need to bolt in a hurry. It is not necessarily reflective of the environment you provide for her or of the actual presence of any predators in your home.

As a natural prey animal for many different species for millions of generations, your cat is inherently hard-wired to respond to changes in the environment without the benefit of evaluating the actual threat first. For cats, the rule tends to be: react first and assess the danger second. You have undoubtedly seen evidence of this innate jumpiness either in your cat, cats you have seen out and about in the zeitgeist, or in popular videos online.

Though inborn in the feline species, this hyper-alertness brings with it a significant amount of stress, especially if triggered too often. Stress triggers the release of harmful hormones like cortisol and adrenaline into the bloodstream. Such hormonal releases can increase blood pressure and blood glucose and can also suppress immune and digestive functioning.

As you can imagine, higher stress levels can be tough on the internal organs. Enter your senior cat, whose organs are already battling the deterioration of aging. Now consider how his senses and cognition are declining, carrying the potential for surprises around every corner. Also, like humans, as we age, his tolerance for irritants in his environment is diminishing as well.

Tip #89: Keep calm energy in your home for your senior cat.

His body cannot afford to deal with excess environmental stressors. You can help him cope with the stress in his environment by keeping calm energy in your home, minimizing excessive noise and activity. Keep routines consistent and predictable.

Provide warmth for his aging body. Many elder felines appreciate heating pads and thermal blankets to battle the physical stress that comes with a human ambient temperature that tends to be cool for feline tastes.

Cats as Predators

On the other end of the prey and predator spectrum, being a predator living in a domestic situation brings its own source of stress. Many people believe, mistakenly, that elder cats want to sleep all the time. The truth is that most cats, including senior and geriatric cats, suffer from boredom, as their environmental stimulation is not on par with what they would encounter in a wild situation.

Tip #90: Actively stimulate your senior cat's prey drive to keep her mind sharp and decrease the stress that comes from boredom.

Do not believe the myth that your senior kitty has increased sleep needs. Instead, help her stay vital, lively, and vibrant by giving her a home environment that is full of enriching stimuli. It is, of course, essential to consider any physical limitations her advanced age might cause, but you can still stimulate her prey drive with interactive play.

You may find that you need to be the play instigator, as your older cat will not likely invent her own fun like she would have done in her younger years. You may find that the more you play with her, though, the more she wants to play – and she may revert to devising her own games when she's feeling particularly frisky.

Do not simply leave her to her own devices, though. Continue to play with her, or she will likely go back to a more sedentary lifestyle. You may need to access your creativity to develop ways to encourage and engage the prey drive in your elder feline buddy.

Just like human seniors in nursing homes, even when their mobility is limited, they still benefit from stimulation and playtime. Provide fun things to investigate and keep the environment novel to stimulate all of her senses. Items like boxes and bags to explore, tissue paper to act as hunting blinds that make interesting rustling sounds, and cat herbs like catnip, silver vine, and valerian can all provide entertainment and activate feline senses.

If your cat has a favorite treat – especially the kind that has a strong odor – dropping pieces of that treat around the house for her to find can be an enriching activity. It stimulates her innate foraging instincts. If you notice that she does not locate the treats readily, it's okay. You can simply let her watch you drop them so that she follows you around and picks them up. It's still an activity that enhances her day.

The Behavior Change Bottom Line

Tip #91: Give your aging cat the benefit of the doubt in terms of behavior changes.

Some cat parents write off changes as "bad" behavior or simply age-related and therefore not treatable. However, there is always a reason, and it can often be treated or managed. As your kitty's guardian and advocate, it is up to you to find out why she is behaving differently. Seek understanding first before overreacting with corrective actions.

She deserves the benefit of the doubt and the opportunity to fix or reverse the problems behind those deviations from the norm. Whatever kind of change you notice, a veterinary visit is in order first to help determine the cause. The bond between you and your elder feline friend is at stake, and so are her health and potential longevity.

Senior Cat Nutrition

Tip #92: Proper nutrition is the foundation for health at all stages and is especially important for a senior cat to maintain healthy organ function.

The most important thing to remember for nutrition at all stages of life is that the quality of the diet and how it interacts with the body carries more value than any brand name or even any type of food. For example, a high protein and low carbohydrate formulation help build lean muscle mass, and as cats often lose lean muscle mass as part of their aging process, it remains imperative for older cats. It may, in fact, be even more essential.

One potential caveat involving dietary protein is that specific diagnoses common to senior cats – kidney disease, for example – manifest in a reduced ability for the feline body to process protein properly. As a result, many traditional veterinarians will recommend a low-protein veterinary-only prescription diet for kitties with kidney disease.

While I am not a veterinarian, and I am not here to contradict any veterinary professionals, I tend to side with holistic medical practitioners who are more likely to recommend a more species-appropriate diet throughout the cat's life cycle to avoid systemic organ diseases in the first place.

I recommend seeking a second opinion from a holistic or integrative veterinarian before settling immediately for the prescription diet your traditional veterinarian may endorse, even after receiving a diagnosis that might, on the surface, seem to call for a veterinary prescription diet. A cat's body has evolved to use nutrients that would be encountered in a natural setting in the most efficient way to keep the cat healthy. Unfortunately, cat food companies do not always formulate their products accordingly and are often more concerned with their bottom line than with the health of the end consumer.

Once you have discussed nutrition with your aging feline friend's entire health care team, you can make a more informed decision about how to move forward. However, do keep in mind that whatever diet you choose, it should be a high-quality formula that is easy for your kitty to digest and assimilate.

It should also have a high moisture content to support your cat's kidney function since kidney disease does tend to run high in older kitties. Additionally, because cats, having evolved from desert-dwellers whose primary source of moisture came from the prey they ate, often do not drink enough water.

Continue giving your aging kitty frequent small meals to assist natural digestive processes. Ideally, a total of 200 to 250 calories (also known as kcalories in animal nutrition parlance) of high-quality food divided into four to five feedings will most closely replicate a cat's typical feeding patterns that would naturally include rodents, lizards, insects, birds, and other small creatures in the absence of human intervention.

Giving Medications

Your cat's entire health care team is instrumental in determining which kinds of dietary supplements and medications would be most beneficial for him. Unfortunately, some cat parents feel so intimidated by the prospect of trying to give medicines to their feline children that they balk at the idea and refuse to try, or they even avoid seeking medical care in the first place to avoid the unpleasantness they anticipate.

Tip #93: Even if the idea of medicating your cat feels intimidating, remember that there are options available to help accomplish the task.

Such fearful attitudes require reevaluation, especially in the modern age of medicine. If you have these kinds of concerns, please discuss them with your health care practitioners. Compounding pharmacies are skilled in creating medicine formulas that may be tolerable or even enjoyable to the feline palate. If your cat rejects one flavor, they likely have another that she will accept more readily.

Some prescriptions can come in the form of a transdermal ointment. With these types of medicines, you simply rub a small amount inside your kitty's ear where the hair is thin or non-existent, and it is absorbed through the skin. If you can get your cat's medication in this form, it is an effortless alternative to trying to get her to ingest something she may or may not like.

If the treatment is available only in pill or capsule form, do your best to make the process easier on both you and your cat. Try to seek out options that can be done less frequently. For example, knowing that pills and capsules can be difficult to swallow and can get stuck in the throat, try adding a slippery edible substance like a tiny amount of butter to the outside to coat it and make it slip down more easily; then add a small dollop to the end of your cat's nose to encourage her to lick and swallow reflexively.

This is when you will be happy with the decision you made early in your cat's life and/or introduction to your home to mat train her. If she knows that good things often happen in that spot, she will be much more tolerant of any "negative" activities that occur there because of the prospect that something great is in her near future.

Chapter 6 Review:

- Cats enter the senior portion of their lives at around the age of 10 years, and you can consider your cat geriatric or a "super-senior" around 15 years or so.
- When cats enter the twilight of their lives, they make great companions, but their health care requirements increase as their bodies, minds, and senses deteriorate.
- Your cat's health care team can help your cat maintain a stellar quality of life with therapies, nutritional recommendations, and supplements to alleviate the negative effects of the aging process.
- You play a prominent role in your aging friend's quality of life as you provide an environment that is both forgiving and accommodating of the increased needs of advancing age.

- Each cat is an individual and will have unique needs in terms of nutrition and medications to prolong a high quality of life. Work closely with an integrative feline health care team to develop a formula that works for your cat and you.

Chapter 7: Life Cycle Care – End of Life

Bereavement

The unfortunate part of loving and sharing your life with other beings with shorter lifespans than your own is facing the likely heartbreak of someday losing them. As previously discussed, in the absence of unforeseen circumstances, cats have a natural life span that is roughly one-third to one-fifth the length of a natural human life span.

Depending on your age and the age of your cat when you begin rooming with your feline companion, the odds are high that someday you will need to say goodbye to her. Recognizing and accepting the reality that facing the end of life is an inevitable part of life – and when possible, coming to terms with it long before the loss – can go a long way toward your future comfort and healing potential.

The Bonds We Share

Why does the prospect of losing your cat create such intense emotional distress – is there something wrong with you? The answer to this question is resounding, "NO! There is nothing wrong with you." In fact, regardless of what some in human society might want to lead you to believe, what you are feeling is absolutely natural and normal. Being devoid of emotion when faced with this eventuality might be more cause for concern than having heightened anxiety regarding it.

Tip #94: Recognize the significant impact of the human-animal bond on your emotional attachment to your cat.

We all experience different kinds of bonds with our companion cats – and the bond we share with one cat will likely be different from one we share with another, depending on the memories built, the stage of life represented, and a variety of other factors. For some people, the cat is the only consistent being in their lives, alternately taking on the companionship role of child, best friend, parent, confidante, or even something akin to a spouse – obviously without the romantic component.

Our cats live in the moment, accepting us for what and who we are, without conditions and free from harsh judgments. Unfortunately, most people have few, if any, human relationships that provide such pure acceptance.

Additionally, whether traveling through a lifetime together or a relatively short time, we may share deep and personal experiences with our animal companions that we have never, or could never, share with human companions or acquaintances. The relationship often runs more deeply than with the humans in our lives – or even more deeply than we realize or acknowledge until we are faced with loss or begin to recognize the potential for loss.

It only makes sense that when faced with the foreseeable end of our cat's earthly presence, we might feel a depth of despair that baffles a significant segment of human society who may never have succumbed to feline love in the first place. Nevertheless, the pain and damage to the psyche are real, and so is our need to acknowledge and express our feelings about the newly-created deficit in our lives.

Truths Regarding Bereavement

Furthermore, everyone experiences the mourning process differently, and each grief we face throughout our lifetime will be unique as well. It might be comforting if there were a prescribed, linear, one-size-fits-all grieving process that we could expect, and furthermore, if all people underwent the same journey, that is not a realistic expectation. It's not practical for us to expect of ourselves, and it is not realistic for others to expect it of us either.

Tip #95: When mourning the loss of your cat, follow your own grief path and don't let others dictate for you how you "should" be feeling.

The truth is that the people around us – friends, family, and acquaintances, are living a different life and having a different experience than the one we are living and cannot dictate our feelings for us. People tend to be uncomfortable with the intense roller-coaster of emotions the bereaved suffer and will often try to minimize their discomfort in various ways that unintentionally intensify the pain for the grieving.

Some well-meaning people try to dismiss the depth of the feelings of loss with phrases like, "He's in a better place now." However, regardless of your beliefs about the afterlife, your loss is tangible, and your pain is real, whether he is in a better place or not. What you are feeling is his absence, and such platitudes do not change that fact for you.

Others might try to deny that you're even experiencing an actual loss and say things like, "It was only a cat. Just go get another one." I'm here to tell you that what you are feeling is valid and genuine, regardless of the species of the soul you are missing and the availability of another member of the same species to live in your home with you.

Tip #96: For support, consider reaching out to a therapist or a community of others who have experienced similar losses.

Resources are available to help you through your bereavement process. It is not unreasonable to seek talk therapy either online or in person. Support groups are available online for people mourning the loss of companion animals, and some communities even have in-person support groups explicitly geared toward this kind of grief.

An internet search such as "pet loss grief support" should yield beneficial results. In addition, some national and online resources are listed in the "Resources" section of this book as well.

Pre-Grieving and the Hospice Stage

Tip #97: As you begin recognizing the approaching end of your cat's life, preparing yourself for the difficulty to come can help to soften the blow.

The more you can prepare yourself ahead of time, the more it can help your healing process, so if possible, give yourself the space to get ready for the impending loss. Of course, that doesn't mean it will be easy, but pre-grieving over time can help your heart get used to the idea and make the experience more gentle and peaceful for both you and your cat when the moment arrives.

When you know – or sense – the end is near, even if you cannot change the outcome, you can focus on your positive experiences with your cat in the present. Unfortunately, humans seem to be the only animals with the tendency to focus attention on either the past or future.

Non-human animals, including cats, live in the present and generally have a healthier attitude and easier acceptance toward concepts such as death and dying than we do. However, like humans, they do grieve the loss of cherished companions.

Because we tend to live in the past and look toward the future, we human animals are far more likely to try to prolong the process of our loved ones' transitioning from earthly form than are our non-human animal counterparts. We know how much it will hurt, and we want to procrastinate that feeling.

Quite frankly, this author believes that attitude and behavior can make the transition process more painful and difficult for those we love and face losing. Therefore, we owe it to our cats to allow them to leave when they are ready, even though it's painful for us.

Tip #98: Use the hospice stage as a special time to bond with your cat.

Living in the present with your cat will be a gift for both of you, strengthening your bond and bringing you both an intensified sense of joy and gratitude for the time you have left to spend together. So be present with your cat. Focus on making her as comfortable as possible and concentrate on the love between you to make the most of your remaining time.

If you are giving your cat medical treatments, even those that may be unpleasant for you both, you can use the time for bonding. Focus on transmitting positive energy. Talk to her soothingly, whether aloud or internally. Cats are highly intuitive and pick up on our energies in a way that most humans do not sense. As a result, she will feel the love you are sending her.

Take note of your sensory inputs during your time together. For example, note the feel of your cat's fur, her expressions when she looks into your eyes, the sounds she makes, the rumble of her purr. Talk to her and pay attention to her responses.

Snuggle with her. Play with her gently if she is still able to manage it. Create special rituals unique to the two of you for bonding and love.

Give her a lot of her favorite treats and treatments. Remember that once she has passed the point of possible recovery, the quality of your time together is far more important than the quantity, so spoil her with the things she loves, even if that means unhealthful treats. Attune yourself with her soul and be open to feeling her presence after her passing.

Be compassionate with yourself as you prepare for the end and let the grief happen and progress naturally. Too much focus on the unfairness of the situation diminishes the healing potential, while acceptance can be therapeutic. Acceptance doesn't mean you have to like your loss, but it does help you heal from it, even if you still feel the pain.

You may be surprised to learn that veterinary hospice services are available, just like those for human medicine. Such services provide palliative care or comfort for your cat's final stages of life and will also provide you with bereavement resources.

***Tip #99: Consider finding a hospice service that
specializes in companion animals.***

They are not as readily available for animals as they are for humans,
but an internet search may provide you with information about a
hospice service in your local area. They are more common than
many people realize.

Euthanasia

A component that often adds to the emotional weight of facing the
end of your cherished cat friend's journey on earth is having the
direct responsibility for decision-making on his behalf. It can be so
challenging to know whether your decisions are in his best interest
or not. That lack of knowledge can foster an inordinate amount of
self-imposed guilt and self-doubt, adding extra stress to an already
emotionally charged situation.

You are likely to have many questions in regard to helping him
cross over from this life to whatever happens after his passing. It's
very easy to experience anxiety about such weighty decisions.

You may have questions such as, "is my cat's quality of life
diminished enough to warrant putting him out of his misery?"

"Would he ask me to help him transition out of this life if he could
speak to me in my language?"

"Is he in pain?"

"Could he recover from this or could we extend his life significantly
enough to make it worth heroic measures? Or would that just
prolong his suffering?"

"Will I be able to tell when it is time to let go?"

"Am I only holding on for my own benefit?"

When our emotions are already so jumbled, having questions like these swirling around in our heads can make the decision that much more confusing and complicated. Unfortunately, there are often no easy answers to these questions. Each situation is different, and I cannot tell you when it is the right time to help your friend transition or if you should do so at all.

Tip #100: Consult your veterinary team to help you with informed choices and take cues from your cat to help you make the best decisions. Decision-making is best when it's a team effort between affected parties.

Your veterinary team can help you determine when the time may be right to choose euthanasia. They can give you vital information about your kitty's chances for recovery and the potential for quality of remaining life.

Additionally, strange as it may seem to you, ask your cat to let you know when he is ready. He may not be able to tell you in plain English what he wants, but cats are highly intuitive and can be quite communicative if you pay close attention. If you are in tune with him and open to communication, he can help you make those critical decisions on his behalf.

Tip #101: When choosing euthanasia, minimize stress as much as possible. Usually, your kitty's home environment is the least stressful place for the procedure if it is possible to do it there.

If and when you decide that it is time to help him on his end-of-life journey, please consider doing so in the gentlest way possible. Cats are most comfortable in their own homes, and minimizing stress for you and your feline friend is warranted in this situation.

In some cases, your cat's veterinary team may be willing to schedule an appointment outside regular business hours to come to your home to perform euthanasia. However, it's not necessarily common for a traditional general practitioner to do this.

However, if you have built a strong personal relationship and you can be flexible with the time, you may be able to persuade them to do so. It can be comforting and easier on both of you to have familiar faces, hands, and scents surrounding you and your kitty for this important transitional time.

If your veterinarian or holistic practitioner is unable or unwilling to come to your home, most communities have a surprising number of mobile veterinarians who will perform the procedure. Most of them specialize in euthanasia and are well-versed in making the process easy and peaceful for all involved parties.

Chapter 7 Review:

- Losing a companion animal as opposed to a human loved one comes with a unique set of challenges related to societal pressures and expectations. However, what you are feeling is authentic and valid regardless of the reactions you may encounter from other people.
- If you are in the position to anticipate the upcoming loss of your feline friend, allowing yourself some therapeutic pre-grieving before it transpires can help smooth your transition from living together to a new life without your cat. That doesn't mean a kitty's passing will not be painful for you, but some pre-grieving can help make the process healthier and easier to bear when the time comes to say goodbye.
- When confronting the inevitable end of your cat's life, be gentle with yourself and focus on making her as comfortable as possible. Be present with your cat and concentrate on the love between you to make the most of your remaining time.
- Challenged with the need to make crucial decisions such as whether and when to euthanize your cat can be especially traumatic due to the additional weight of self-doubt regarding your choices. Every situation is different. Your veterinarian and your cat can also play a role in helping you decide the best path.
- Resources are available online and in your community to help you with hospice care, at-home euthanasia, and bereavement.

Resources

Source	Purpose	Resource
Alley Cat Allies	Found Cat Socialization Continuum Chart	www.alleycat.org/resources/cat-socialization-continuum-guide
ASPCA Poison Control	Poison Control Hotline	(888)426-4435
ASPCA Poison Control	Poison Information Resource	https://www.aspca.org/pet-care/animal-poison-control
ASPCA Poison Control	Toxic and Non-Toxic Plants (With Photos)	https://www.aspca.org/pet-care/animal-poison-control/toxic-and-non-toxic-plants
Care Credit	Financial Assistance: Veterinary Credit Card with 0% Interest if Paid off Within Term Period	https://www.carecredit.com/
Scratch Pay	Financial Assistance: Short-Term High Approval Rate Patient Financing	https://scratchpay.com/
American Veterinary Medical Association	Animal Guardian Information Resource	https://www.avma.org/resources-tools/pet-owners
American Animal Hospital Association (AAHA)	Animal Guardian Information Resource with Locator Tool	https://www.aaha.org/
Cat Friendly	Cat Friendly Home Page - Browse Page for Info and Search	https://catfriendly.com/

	for Local Cat Friendly Practitioners	
American Association of Feline Practitioners	Cat Guardian Resource and Local Feline-Friendly Practice Locator Resource	https://catvets.com/
Fear Free	Fear Free Home Page - Browse Page for Info and Search for Local Fear-Free Practitioners	https://fearfreepets.com/
Tufts University Veterinary Nutritionists "Petfood-ology" Page	Clinical Nutrition Information for Animal Guardians	https://vetnutrition.tufts.edu/petfoodology/
Association of American Feed Control Officials	Consumer Information About AAFCO and Food Labeling	https://www.aafco.org/Consumers
Caticles	Feline Nutrition Information and Blog	https://www.caticles.com/
Feline Nutrition Foundation	Feline Nutrition Information and Blog	http://feline-nutrition.org/
Balance It	Homemade Cat Food Recipe Resource Tool	https://secure.balanceit.com/ez/index.php?rotator=NewEz
Health and Veterinary Nutritionist Recommendations	Nutrition Information Resource	https://Healthypets.mercola.com
Tufts University Veterinary Nutritionists	Nutrition Information Resource	https://vetnutrition.tufts.edu/
American Association of Feline Practitioners	Information About Positive	https://catvets.com/guidelines/position-

	Reinforcement Training	statements/positive-reinforcement
Feline Behavior Solutions	Information About Positive Reinforcement Training	https://felinebehaviorsolutions.com/use-positive-reinforcement-good-cat-behavior/
Humane Society of Huron Valley	Information About Positive Reinforcement Training	https://www.hshv.org/training-cats-with-positive-reinforcement/
The International Veterinary Academy of Pain Management	Identifying and Understanding Feline Pain/Discomfort	https://ivapm.org/category/feline/
The International Veterinary Academy of Pain Management	Identifying Feline Pain/Discomfort	https://ivapm.org/assess-felines-pain-level/
Sylvester.ai Cell Phone Application	Identifying Presence of Feline Pain/Discomfort	Find in your phone service app store
Pet MD	Info About Feline Acupuncture	https://www.petmd.com/cat/wellness/evr_ct_acunpuncture_for_cats
Wag Walking	Info About Feline Acupuncture	https://wagwalking.com/cat/treatment/acupuncture
Animal Wellness Magazine	Info About Feline Red-Light Therapy	https://animalwellnessmagazine.com/light-therapy-for-dogs-and-cats/
Platinum Therapy Lights Blog	Info About Feline Red-Light Therapy	https://platinumtherapylights.com/blogs/news/red-light-therapy-for-animals

The Purrington Post	Info About Feline Reiki	https://www.thepurringtonpost.com/reiki-and-cats
Path With Paws Blog	Practical Info About Red Light Therapy for Cats for Kidney Failure, Incontinence, and Arthritis	https://pathwithpaws.com/blog/2012/10/20/infrared-light-therapy-for-kidney-failure-incontinence-and-arthritis-in-dogs-and-cats/
TVCOGECO newsmagazine program	Video Showing Feline Reiki in Practice in a Shelter Setting	https://www.youtube.com/watch?v=UNa6dfLa_yw
American Association of Feline Practitioners	End of Life Educational Toolkit	https://catvets.com/public/PDFs/Toolkit/EOL/AAFP-End-of-Life-Toolkit-Full.pdf
Cornell University College of Veterinary Medicine	Grief Support Hotline	607-218-7457
Companion Animal Grief Support Center	Grief Support Resource	www.RainbowsBridge.com
ASPCA End of Life Care Info	Hospice and End-of-Life Resource	www.ASPCA.org/care

About the Expert

Crystal Rector, raised in a feline-loving family, has studied cats since early childhood. Spending her spare time with the many barn cats on the farm where she was raised, she dreamed for years that one day she would photograph them for a living, but instead found herself working in various roles within the veterinary industry for a collective ten years.

Opportunities to take care of veterinary client animals laid the foundation for what would eventually become her full-time business in the Phoenix, Arizona area as Crystal the Pet Nanny. Although she takes care of all kinds of animals, Crystal is a feline specialist and has an exceptional affinity for cats, with particular interest in behavior and enrichment. This interest led her to earn the Diploma of Distinction in Feline Behavior and Psychology from the Centre of Excellence.

She shares her life with her husband Sean, who keeps her from becoming a crazy cat collector, her dog Stella, a fish she calls "Fishy Friend", and her beautiful cat Josie – who is queen of all she surveys.

HowExpert publishes quick 'how to' guides on all topics from A to Z by everyday experts. Visit HowExpert.com to learn more.

Recommended Resources

- HowExpert.com – Quick 'How To' Guides on All Topics from A to Z by Everyday Experts.
- HowExpert.com/free – Free HowExpert Email Newsletter.
- HowExpert.com/books – HowExpert Books
- HowExpert.com/courses – HowExpert Courses
- HowExpert.com/clothing – HowExpert Clothing
- HowExpert.com/membership – HowExpert Membership Site
- HowExpert.com/affiliates – HowExpert Affiliate Program
- HowExpert.com/jobs – HowExpert Jobs
- HowExpert.com/writers – Write About Your #1 Passion/Knowledge/Expertise & Become a HowExpert Author.
- HowExpert.com/resources – Additional HowExpert Recommended Resources
- YouTube.com/HowExpert – Subscribe to HowExpert YouTube.
- Instagram.com/HowExpert – Follow HowExpert on Instagram.
- Facebook.com/HowExpert – Follow HowExpert on Facebook.